Diana Kerr and Heather Wilkinson

# Providing Good Care at Night for Older People

## Practical Approaches for Use in Nursing and Care Homes

Jessica Kingsley *Publishers*
London and Philadelphia

'Unselving: for those who suffer and those who care' reprinted with permission from Clancy 2000
Table 3.1 reprinted with permission from Knauth and Hornberger 2003
'Sleep hygiene chart' reprinted with permission from Shapiro *et al.* 1997
Figure 4.1 reprinted with permission from Dementia Services Development Centre 1997
Figure 7.2 reprinted with permission from Bupa 2009
Figure 7.3 reprinted with permission from Joint Surrey and Borders Partnership NHS Trust and Dietetic Project
Figure 9.1 reprinted with permission from Meredith 2009
Figure 9.2 reprinted with permission from Bell *et al.* 2004
'Night-time care prompts: Guidance for inspectors of care homes' reprinted with permission from Care Quality Commission 2009.
Figure 10.1 reprinted with permission from Dementia Services Development Centre 1997


First published in 2011
by Jessica Kingsley Publishers
116 Pentonville Road
London N1 9JB, UK
and
400 Market Street, Suite 400
Philadelphia, PA 19106, USA
*www.jkp.com*

**Library of Congress Cataloging in Publication Data**
A CIP catalog record for this book is available from the Library of Congress

**British Library Cataloguing in Publication Data**
A CIP catalogue record for this book is available from the British Library


ISBN 978 1 84905 064 7


Printed and bound in Great Britain by
MPG Books Group

# Contents

# Acknowledgements

We owe thanks to a number of people who gave us their time and the benefit of their knowledge and experience.

Graham Jackson gave us invaluable help on the chapter on medication, Rose Gordon on issues around end-of-life care, and David McNair on the use of lighting. As ever, Annabelle Meredith provided enthusiasm and ideas. Kim McDougall and the senior night staff at North Lanarkshire Council showed what could be done easily and cheaply. Kathryn Dunne for carrying out the laborious task of proofreading. Chris Lawes for the eagle eye and critical comment.

We would also like to thank the Joseph Rowntree Foundation for funding the research out of which this book grew.

Finally, lots of thanks go to Matty and Brian who have shown forbearance in the face of our endless moans and hours at the computer.

# Introduction

Most research and information about residential and nursing homes (referred to as care homes throughout this book) focus on the daytime (Kerr, Wilkinson and Cunningham 2008). This book is written in acknowledgment of the need to bring night-time and night care into focus so that it can be given the same level of interest, support, inspection and research as the daytime. If this is to happen, night-time must be seen as an integral and significant part of the whole 24 hours of the day. There needs to be a greater understanding of the experiences of night staff and of the night-time culture as well as the experiences and night-time needs of residents and patients in care homes.

Care homes are not inspected with the same rigour at night as they are in the day (Kerr *et al.* 2008). Relatives and potential residents make their decisions about where someone should live based on what they see in the day. They look at the activities, the staff and the environment of the day and use that information to inform their decisions about the quality and appropriateness of a place. The experience of the daytime place cannot automatically be assumed to be the experience of the night-time place. The night can and often does have a different culture, different staffing, different resources and different needs of the residents and patients. Night-time care must be properly resourced and managed. This will not be the case until night staff receive the same level of training, knowledge, skills, resources and supervision as day staff.

This book is intended to provide night staff, their managers and inspectors of services with information, knowledge and skills that will help towards the provision of positive night-time care.

Much that is in this book is also relevant to daytime staff and this is not unexpected. There is clearly an interrelationship between night and day care. Things that happen in the day will often affect the night, and things that are important to night care are usually equally important to day care. The intention in this book is not to portray night care as something separate and disengaged from day care, but to highlight the need to give more emphasis to night care and to pay particular attention to those aspects of night care that are different from daytime provision and practice.

Case study material has been used throughout the book to help illustrate key issues and to enable the reader to identify with the problems and challenges that the examples present. These case studies are all based on real examples.

The book can be read sequentially, but it is also anticipated that readers will dip into it and use the various chapters as stand-alone guides to specific practice issues.

Chapter 1 sets out the culture, atmosphere and care at night-time in care homes and highlights how the differences between night and day impact upon the care needs of residents and the care practices of night staff.

Chapter 2 focuses on the concerns and needs of staff working nights. It includes the necessary legal definitions concerning night work.

Chapter 3 goes on to explore some of the potential ill-health risks incurred by night shift workers. It then identifies ways of minimising the potential ill effects by providing strategies that can be used by managers and staff.

Chapter 4 describes the most common dementias and gives a basic introduction to the brain and its functions. This is followed by a consideration of the impact and experience of dementia for residents and staff in care homes. This chapter then goes on to identify how staff can better respond to the person with dementia at night.

Chapter 5 explores the issue of sleep. The nature of normal sleep amongst older people is detailed, followed by a consideration of those things that disturb sleep, particularly amongst people in care homes. Suggestions of how to improve sleep are then given.

Chapter 6 examines the care practice of 'checking' at night and recommends ways in which this practice can be more effective and less intrusive. This chapter also goes on to explore the issue of continence as this has a significant bearing on the need to check residents.

Chapter 7 tackles the issue of eating and drinking and highlights how the night can be a time to promote good nutrition.

Chapter 8 describes how the physical environment can promote or negatively affect night-time care. Examples are given of ways to improve the night-time environment, including the use of assistive technology.

Chapter 9 focuses on activities that can be effective and engaging during the evening and night-time. This chapter contains many practical suggestions.

Chapter 10 concentrates on pain and how ineffective pain diagnosis and management can have a detrimental effect on sleep. Strategies are given to improve night-time pain relief.

Chapter 11 links closely to Chapter 10 and outlines the key issues relating to medication and night-time care.

Chapter 12 gives attention to the dying process and night-time care, and recommends ways of supporting the dying person, other residents, relatives and staff.

Chapters 13 highlights the importance and needs of relatives in relation to night-time care.

Chapter 14 places the spotlight on guidelines for inspectors of night-time care. The guidelines are also seen as a useful tool for managers to help focus on night-time requirements and so evaluate night-time practices in their homes.

# Chapter 1

# The Night-Time

Before addressing the various topics covered in this book, it is important to pause and think about the nature and significance of night-time, both generally and in the context of care homes. Night-time and daytime are different. When we want to express how different things are from each other we often say 'they are like night and day'. In a care home this difference is very evident.

In the daytime people come and go: there are staff changeovers and doctors' visits; activities coordinators arrive; prospective residents and their relatives visit; the cook arrives, the tradesmen come in, the gardener is at work; managers are around; and some residents go out and come back in again. The outside world comes in throughout the day. At night the door is shut against the world. After the night staff have arrived there are far fewer people around and much less coming and going. The night staff are to a substantial extent separated from the world outside.

The night-time has a culture and atmosphere different from that of the day. Night-time is often when fears and worries can take hold. The night hours seem longer than the day hours. The night-time, which can be a time of slumber and peace, can also be the time of fear and turmoil. How often do we wake in the morning to find the fears of the night to be gone or at least diminished? In the still of the night the concept of time can change: it dislocates, it fools and extends. The anchors and cues of the daytime are gone and the night-time ticks slowly. For all of us this can present problems, but for people with dementia the night can be particularly dislocating and confusing.

For many older people it is rare to sleep continuously throughout the night. The night can be punctuated by fretful periods of waking, perhaps because of pain or anxieties about failing health and fears for the future.

For people with dementia the stillness and emptiness of the night can be particularly frightening and disorientating. Dementia takes people back in time. They need cues and help to orientate. Alone, at night, there are few, if any. Someone with dementia can be trapped in the past, unable to understand the present. The damage to the circadian rhythm – the mechanism that regulates our body clock, telling us the difference between daytime and night-time – means that people with dementia will often misinterpret or mistrust such night-time cues as do exist. Often, if they wake, people will assume it is morning and time for the tasks of the new day rather than the task of the night-time – that is, to sleep.

Joseph Clancy captures this dislocation so well in his poem 'Unselving: for those who suffer and those who care' when he writes:

> He wakes to find the bed
> Half empty. She has gone
>
> Past midnight, in her nightgown,
> Four streets and eighteen years astray.
>
> A policeman brings her home.
> He leads her back to bed.
>
> He holds her, sobbing till she sleeps. (Clancy 2000)

The disorientation brought on by dementia means, as illustrated here, that the conviction that the night has passed can be so strong that any contradictory cues that do exist are often ignored.

### CASE STUDY 1

A man, with dementia, always got up at 7 a.m. to go to work. Because of the effect of his dementia, when he woke at 3 a.m. he assumed it really must be 7 a.m. and time for work. Undaunted by the fact that the clock showed 3 a.m., he decided that the timepiece was wrong and he was right. He then changed the hands of the clock to 7 o'clock. Perhaps he just wanted the night to end. One way to deal with the fears of the night-time might be to speed it up and get to the daytime as quickly as possible!

Generally, however, despite the needs of people at night and the specific needs of people with dementia, services still continue to provide night-time care and support as if the night-time were a time when people were more or less continually asleep, not distressed and not in need of reassurance.

## What are nights like in a care home?

The following is provided not as a description of any one particular home but as a generalised picture. The intention is to provide the reader, who may not have worked nights in a care home, with a sense of the main characteristics of a typical night. Of course, this is given with the caveat that there are probably rarely two nights or two homes the same.

Between 7 o'clock and 9 o'clock in the evening there will, usually, be a shift change. Day staff start to finish up, which may involve some residents being put to bed and others being prepared for bed. Usually this will only be a small proportion of the total resident group. There will then be a handover meeting between the two shifts. Often this will be between the most senior staff from each shift, with other members of staff in attendance. The latter is not always the case; often it is just the most senior staff – probably the nurses on duty or the most senior care staff if there are no nurses.

Once all of the night staff are on duty, the night-time routine begins. This may involve the provision of a hot drink and a snack, such as a biscuit, after which the process of getting people to bed begins. This involves walking people to their bedrooms or transferring them to wheelchairs to take them to bed. Those who require assistance with washing and changing to nightclothes will be helped; others will do this themselves. People who require continence pads will be attended to. People will also be given any medication that is required.

Although most people will probably be in bed by 10.30 p.m., there will be some residents who may not want to go to bed, and they may stay up for another hour or more. There may be a few residents who will stay up much of the night.

Depending on the regime in the home, there will be a routine around 'checking'. Ideally this will be carried out with clear guidelines based on individual assessments of need. It may well be, however, that there will be a routine that involves regular checking of everyone.

During the night some people will get up and walk about, some will get up for the toilet, some will become distressed and require comforting, some will require food and drink. There will also be residents whose illnesses require medical intervention. Night-time is also when people are most likely to die.

At around 6 o'clock the morning routine will begin. This may involve another check of people's continence pads. It will also involve helping some early risers to get up. Other people may simply require assistance to go to the toilet and will then return to bed. Some will require help with washing and others may require an early breakfast snack.

Day staff will usually arrive between 7 and 9 a.m., depending on the home's regime. There will then be another handover meeting and the night staff will leave. (Taken from Kerr *et al.* 2008, pp.12–13.)

It is this world that this book is about.

## Summary

The culture, atmosphere and care at night-time in care homes can be significantly different from the daytime. Evenings and nights are quieter, less busy. There are fewer staff and usually no visitors, and as a consequence the night staff and residents may feel very separated from the outside world. Night-time can be a time when fears and worries take hold. For people living in care homes, especially those with dementia, the night can be a confusing time as the clues and cues of the daytime are gone.

# Chapter 2

# Night Staff: Their Work and Experiences

This book is about providing good care at night for older people in care homes. It is not possible to separate the provision of good care of the residents/patients from good care of staff. If staff are stressed, unhealthy, anxious, under-resourced, poorly trained and/or under-managed, then this will have an obvious and inevitable effect on their interactions with the people in their care. For this reason the next two chapters of this book will consider the experiences and health status of night staff. First, it is important to be clear about the definition of who constitutes a night worker and indeed what is meant, legally, by 'night-time'.

## Definition of a night worker

The Working Time Regulations (1998) determined that night workers are classed as those people who work for at least three hours of their shift as a normal course during 'night-time'. The definition of 'normal course' may be given a rather loose interpretation due to the case of R v Attorney General for Northern Ireland, *ex parte* Burns (1999) which held that the directive was not limited to those who only or mainly worked night shifts, but rather applied as long as working night shifts was a regular feature of the employment.

## Definition of night-time

Night-time is a defined term in the Working Time Regulations (WTR) as a period lasting not less than seven hours and which includes between midnight and 5 a.m. The default period for night-time under the WTR is 11 p.m. until 6 a.m., but this may be changed by a collective or workforce agreement to include such times as 10 p.m. to 5 a.m. or midnight to 7 a.m. or any time in between these two bands.

Night workers are essential to the 24-hour care and support that people in care homes require. People who work night shifts will do so for the various benefits they bring. This chapter is about the experience of working at night. This means that it is mainly relevant to people who work exclusively on nights, but it also has relevance to shift workers who are part of a rota system that involves both day and night shifts. The following issues will be addressed:

- the reasons people work at night
- the experience of working at night
- ways to improve night-time work experiences.

## The reasons people work at night

### CASE STUDY 2

Jennifer started to do the night shift in a care home when her husband was ill and needed daytime care. After he died, her mother became ill and Jennifer continued to work at night in order to balance the care needs of her mother and the need for her to work.

After the death of her mother, Jennifer, by now into a routine of night work, decided not to return to day shift. She has now worked at night for 15 years.

People work at night for a variety of reasons. Some people, like Jennifer, find that this is the best or only way that they can balance their various commitments. They often have other caring and family responsibilities that preclude them from working during the daytime. Other people, again like Jennifer, started working nights for the above reasons, but by the time their commitments had changed they were into a routine and a way of life that they no longer wanted to change.

Some people will work nights for a given and predicted short period. Students who use night work as a way of supplementing their student loans or grants are a good example of this. Here the night work is often for months or a few years at most.

Groups of people who find getting other work problematic may work nights. Some people choose night work because they like the control that it gives. Night workers have more autonomy than day workers. Little or no management throughout the night and small teams mean that workers can develop a sense of camaraderie and team spirit.

## The experience of working at night

### CASE STUDY 3

Margaret, Joe and Cynthia work together on the night shift. They always work together unless one of them is off sick, in which case an agency nurse is employed.

The three of them work five or six nights a week. They have worked together now for three years. They feel close to each other and feel that they work very much as a team.

There is, however, no night-time involvement from the manager after 10 p.m. and therefore no supervision or easy access to management when there are problems.

The three of them describe feelings of isolation from the main running of the home. They express feelings of anxiety. They often use the expression 'What if': 'What if someone falls? What if there is an intruder? What if there is a fire? What if someone dies?'

They also feel passed by when it comes to training.

Night work can be very rewarding. Staff often feel that they have more control over their routines. They also often form close-knit small groups where each person plays a well-defined role in the small team. They come to rely on each other in a close and supportive way that may not so easily occur during the day shift.

Night staff do, however, have a number of negative experiences as well, some of which are highlighted in the case study above. Kerr *et al.* (2008) found that staff working at night often felt that they were not given the same attention and acknowledgement as day staff. This led to feelings of isolation and separation from the running of the home and in particular from any decisions made that affected the home and their work.

The feelings of isolation and separation were also compounded by a sense of anxiety. There may be a number of reasons for this, but it is perhaps partly a consequence of the way in which the night affects us all. As stated earlier, night-time can be when fears and worries take hold. In the study carried out by Kerr *et al.* (2008) the anxiety and worry expressed itself in the use of the phrase 'What if'.

In most homes there will be a night manager whose job it is to manage the night shift. The overall manager for the home, however, will not have the same presence throughout the night as she does during the day. Often the senior manager will only be present in the care home during the early evening or early morning. This means that night staff are functioning without the presence and supervision of senior management. This is not in anyway to denigrate the role of night managers. It is, however, a reflection of the fact that the person who knows most about the running of the home and who is responsible for the overall standards, culture and practices within the home has little direct access to night staff; night staff in turn have little access to the overall manager. The lack of direct senior management support can leave night staff with a sense that they are not as valued as day staff (Kerr *et al.* 2008).

The night shift is usually smaller than the day shift, leaving the fewer staff who are on duty with greater individual responsibility. The smaller number on shift also means that people have fewer colleagues with whom they can try ideas or share worries. This is compounded by the fact that there can be a relatively higher proportion of agency and bank staff at night. If there are only three staff on duty and one is from an agency, then one third of the staff is not from the permanent staff list. The greater use of agency staff may well be the consequence of night staff numbers being often 'cut to the bone' (Kerr *et al.* 2008) and higher sickness levels amongst night staff (see Chapter 3). Agency staff require support from regular staff as they rarely know as much about the residents. This puts another burden on the regular staff who are not able to leave work to agency staff with the same level of confidence as they would to their regular colleagues. This can also feed the feeling of anxiety.

The feeling of not being as valued as day staff and of anxiety is compounded by the fact that night staff often receive less training than day staff (Kerr *et al.* 2008). There are a number of reasons why night staff get less training than day staff. A primary cause is undoubtedly because most training is held during the day. It is worth considering how bizarre it would seem to ask day staff to go for training at 3 a.m. when they would expect to be asleep, yet we often expect night staff to go on training courses during the day when they would, routinely, be asleep. Night staff attending training during the day after a night shift or prior to going on a night shift is unacceptable practice and certainly undervalues night staff experiences. It also usually means that even if night staff manage to get through the training session/day, they will have problems with concentration and will generally learn less.

Many training courses tend to focus on daytime activities and issues (Kerr *et al.* 2008), for example, training on continence (this is dealt with in more depth in the section on continence in Chapter 6). If night staff have struggled to get to training, it is important that the training is properly targeted and relevant. Bias towards daytime issues tends to reinforce the sense that night issues are not taken as seriously. This feeling can be reinforced when, as does sometimes happen, night staff are told that if they want to obtain vocational qualifications, they have to move on to day shifts.

The lower levels of training that night staff are offered and can access mean that they can find themselves often having to make decisions without adequate knowledge. This is particularly the case in relation to caring for people with dementia. The lack of training is compounded by a lack of information that new night staff receive. Many people who work at nights have no induction and have to find their way slowly through the various problems and issues that are peculiar to night work.

## Ways to improve night-time work experiences

The isolation and separation from the running of the home that night staff often experience can and should be addressed by enabling them to engage at a number of levels. This is greatly facilitated when staff do day shifts as well as nights. This, of course, is not always an option. For staff who only do nights, there is a need for management to be much more proactive in their engagement. Managers who are in the home in the early evening and the early morning do have some sense of what is going on and do meet the night staff, but these times represent particular phases of the shift and do not provide a complete picture (Kerr *et al.* 2008).

Managers need to meet with night staff in a structured way. This would enable more information to be given, more opportunity for staff to express their concerns and needs, and also, of course, it would enable the visible and actual management of night-time staff. Perhaps the most important thing that needs to happen is for managers to be more involved and, therefore, more aware of what happens throughout the night. This does, of course, happen in many homes but it is not universal. Managers need to make sure staff are aware of emergency procedures. Fire procedures, for example, must be explained and accessible, not tucked away in an office. In relation to training, there is much that needs to be done. All training programmes and especially vocational training programmes must address night-time issues and challenge the assumption that the training given to day staff covers all the relevant night-time issues.

Staff who work nights and attend courses must be given time off. This means that they should not be expected to do a night shift before or after training. Trainers should be encouraged to provide training in the evenings, maybe for 1–2 hours before the night shift starts. This does have cost implications, as it will involve having two groups of staff in at once: either the previous shift has to stay late or the night shift has to come in early. If night staff are to attend day courses, this often requires that the organisation pays them to attend and has the extra cost of employing agency staff if this means that the night staff are unable to do the subsequent night shift.

Where requirements are made in relation to levels and types of qualifications, it is imperative that these explicitly include night staff. Kerr *et al.* (2008) found that where targets for training and qualification levels did not differentiate between day and night workers, the targets were sometimes 'met solely or substantially through the training of day staff' (p.23). It is critical that any such future requirements specifically stipulate night staff training levels and not assume that 'staff' will automatically include all staff, both night and day. It is intolerable and unacceptable that night staff, who are caring for the same residents as day staff, are often given less training.

## Induction training

New night staff often have to find their way around with little or no induction training. A group of senior night staff in North Lanarkshire Council, Scotland, developed a list of things that could be used as an induction procedure for all new night staff to help them get to grips with the routine, the demands and the peculiar culture of the night.

---

### NEW NIGHT STAFF: WHAT YOU NEED TO KNOW ABOUT LOOKING AFTER YOURSELF

- It can take 6–9 months to find your way on night shift.
- Organise your sleep time well and make sure family and friends help you get as much as you need.
- Eat proper food at regular times.
- You can feel sick at times as a new member of staff – so what should you do?
- You might feel sick when you come back from holiday or after having time off.
- Wear loose appropriate clothing. Shoes not too tight as the body can swell at night.
- Have health checks.
- You may have problems with concentration.
- Eye focus may be diminished when trying to carry out IT skills in relation to tasks to be completed.

---

What is interesting about this list is that the staff clearly had important insights and knowledge that needed to be passed on, but this was not done in a routine or systematic way. Most of the things on the list above will be given more substance and discussed further in the following chapters.

# Summary

The formal definition of a night worker is provided through the Working Time Regulations (1998) as someone who works for at least three hours of his shift as a normal course during 'night-time'. The Working Time Regulations also define night-time as a period lasting not less than seven hours and which includes the time between midnight and 5 a.m.

People work nights for various reasons – for example, to balance caring and family commitments or to supplement income. Students often find it a good way to balance working and daytime study requirements; other people find it gives them a level of autonomy that they value.

Night work can be very rewarding, but it can also have a number of negative implications and consequences.

The well-being of staff working at night is critical to the well-being of the people they care for. Staff who are anxious, stressed, unhealthy, underresourced and given insufficient training will struggle to provide good quality care.

Staff working at night often identify a feeling of isolation and separation from the running of the care home. This isolation can lead to feelings of anxiety and uncertainty about some areas of practice. This is compounded by the fact that night staff usually receive less training than day staff, often because training is not provided at times convenient for night staff and often because it is more focused on daytime issues and not sufficiently focused on night-time. In many homes the manager will have much less contact with the night staff and practices. There will also be fewer staff on duty with greater individual responsibility.

Night-time care can be improved with increased management involvement, more targeted and time-appropriate training, and support and clarity around night-time procedures, including emergency procedures.

# Chapter 3

# Night Staff and Their Health

There are many benefits to working at nights. However, there are also some less attractive elements and a few potentially harmful health implications. The intention in this chapter is not to labour these or to discourage people from working at night. It is to ensure that people are made aware and are well informed of the implications of working at night. With the right information they can be prepared to develop strategies to counteract any negative psychological, physical, social, emotional and health experiences wherever possible.

The following issues will be addressed in this chapter:

- the health implications of working at night
- making the night work better: things managers need to consider in developing night work rotas
- making the night work better: things managers and night workers need to address whilst they are on duty
- making the night work better: things night workers need to put in place for themselves after work.

## CASE STUDY 4

Patricia started to do night shifts when she was newly married and new to the country. Her spoken English was not good and she found it hard to get a job. Night work became available. She now speaks fluent English and has worked nights for ten years and is reluctant to move elsewhere. The routine that she and her husband have has become entrenched and neither feels the need to change it.

Patricia has a number of health-related problems either caused or exacerbated by her decision to work at night. She has general digestive problems and in particular suffers with irritable bowel syndrome. Patricia also reports problems with concentration, particularly on her drive home. Socially she often feels isolated from friends and family, especially when there are evening activities that she has to forgo because of her night work.

Patricia's experience is not untypical (Kerr *et al.* 2008). Working shifts does not automatically cause health problems. There are many variables, such as the type of rotation, the age of the workers and the amount of time spent working on shifts. It does appear from research, however, that exclusively working at nights or working lots of nights as part of a shift system does have a detrimental effect on people's health (Costa and Pokorski 2000; International Agency for Research on Cancer 2007; Knutsson 2003).

Working at night means that people are working against their natural circadian rhythm – the way our bodies are programmed to wake in the light of the day and sleep at night when it is dark. This biological clock, as it is often referred to, is responsible for changes in our core body temperature, our sleep–wake patterns and even many emotional, cognitive, psychological and behavioural functions. Our circadian rhythm is particularly important for the production of the hormone melatonin, which is secreted in higher amounts throughout the night whilst we sleep. Melatonin has antioxidant properties, which boost our immune system and, importantly, act to protect us against certain cancers. Inadequate or disturbed sleep, to which night workers are more susceptible, affects the production of melatonin and this then has an impact on the body's ability to suppress the development of some cancers.

There is now mounting evidence of the increased risk faced by shift workers and especially night shift workers of the development of certain cancers such as breast, prostate and possibly colorectal cancer (Davis and Mirick 2006; Hanson 2006). The link between the increased risks of the onset of breast cancer in middle-aged women who have worked long periods of night shift was evidenced by work carried out by the International Agency for Research on Cancer (IARC 2007), a unit of the United Nation's World Health Organization (WHO) which concluded that 'Shift work that involves circadian disruption is probably carcinogenic to humans' (2007, p.1). This link led the Danish government, in March 2009, to make payment of compensation to some women who had developed breast cancer after working night shifts for a long time. Some had worked nights for 30 years. A study carried out in Finland by Lahti *et al.* (2008) found that night-time work predisposed some men to non-Hodgkin's lymphoma.

As indicated above, our immune system is also affected by the lack of sleep. It seems that it is diminished in proportion to the amount of sleep debt (how much sleep we are missing from a normal healthy regime), and this leaves people more susceptible to viral and bacterial infections (Peate 2007). The general debilitating affects of working at night can lead to an increase in 'accidents and may produce health risks such as sleeping or gastro-intestinal disorders, depression, cardio-vascular disease, overweight, and disturbed sexual activity and fertility' (Rüdiger 2004, p.1022).

Davis and Mirick (2006) reported that working night shifts can negatively affect fertility. Links have also been found between working night shifts and an increased risk of preterm birth and low birth weight (Axelsson, Rylander and Molin 1989; Bisanti, Olsen and Basso 1996; McDonald, McDonald and Armstrong 1988; Mammalle, Laumon and Lazar 1984; Nurminen 1989; Uehata and Sasakawa 1982; Xu *et al.* 1994). An increased risk of miscarriage has also been identified (Peate 2007).

In addition to health risks, there are also risks in relation to alertness and concentration. Peate (2007) identified the following impairments amongst staff who are tired and fatigued:

- delayed reaction times
- delayed responses
- delayed thinking
- diminished memory
- failure to respond at appropriate times
- impaired efficiency
- provision of false responses.

One consequence of these impairments is that people who work at night are three times more likely to be involved in a work-related accident than day workers (Swaen *et al.* 2003). Day-shift workers are generally more tired than non-shift workers when they drive home. Night-shift workers, however, appear to experience higher levels of sleepiness and lower levels of driving skills than people doing non-night shifts. (Rogers, Holmes and Spencer 2001).

Of course, this does not mean that all night workers are going to develop all of these difficulties and conditions. The risk is distributed slightly differently amongst different groups of night workers. Some people seem .to be better able to adapt to shift and night work than others (Mason 2008). There are, however, some people who 'should never work nights because they're more vulnerable to deleterious health effects (such as gastrointestinal and cardiac disturbances) when their circadian rhythms are disrupted' (Mason 2008, p.1).

This all sounds rather gloomy and worrying, and suggests that working shifts and particularly nights shifts is not a good idea. This is not necessarily so. It is important, however, to highlight the fact that the link exists and that the research findings must be taken seriously by night workers and their employers. There are strategies and interventions that could lessen some of the risks associated with shift and particularly night-shift work. These must be taken on board and implemented wherever possible if risks are going to be, at least, minimised.

## Making the night work better

Strategies to improve night workers' health and well-being will be addressed under the following three headings:

- things managers need to consider when developing night work rotas
- things managers and night workers need to address whilst they are on duty
- things night workers need to put in place for themselves after work.

## Things managers need to consider when developing night work rotas

Managers need to take account of the effect of night work on staff and look at ways to alleviate or eliminate the negative consequences. It is important that night workers are given the best possible information and support to enable them to continue to work without all of the health, social and skills deficits discussed above. Without the right information, care and support for the night staff, managers put both the workers and the people that they are caring for at risk.

There are a number of things that can reduce some of the short- and long-term effects of working shifts that involve night work. Knauth *et al.* (1983, p.374) point out that whilst there is no single optimum solution, the first thing managers should investigate is 'can the amount of shift work or night work per person be reduced e.g. by shorter working weeks, years or working life or, alternatively, by shift systems including more day work'.

### Shift patterns

There has been some research into the effects of different shifts. Although, as indicated above, there is no single best solution, there are some characteristics and patterns that seem to be better than others. There are many variables that have to be taken into account

## Table 3.1 Ergonomic recommendations regarding the sequence of shifts

| Criterion | Recommendations | Expected effects when the recommendations are fulfilled (↓ reduce, minimize, avoid; ↑ improve) |
|---|---|---|
| **Maximum number of consecutive shifts for:** | | |
| Night shifts | (1) Few night shifts in succession (maximum of 3) | Problems of adaptations of circadian rhythms ↓ Accumulation of sleep deficits ↓ Social contacts ↑ |
| | (2) Avoid permanent night work | Potential long-term health effects ↓ Accumulation of sleep deficits ↓ Social contacts ↑ |
| Morning shifts | (3) Few morning shifts in succession (maximum of 3) | Accumulation of sleep deficits ↓ |
| Evening shifts | (4) Few evening shifts in succession (maximum of 3) | Social contacts ↑ |
| **Direction of rotation** | | |
| MEN = forward rotation, phase delay; NEM = backward rotation, phase advance | (5) Forward rotation | Problems of adaptations of circadian rhythms ↓ |
| **Particular sequence of shifts** | | |
| N–M | (6) At least 2 days off after last night shift | Reduction of sleep before morning shift ↓ |
| N–N | (7) Avoid N–N | Problems of adaptations of circadian rhythms ↓ |
| M–E–N | (8) Avoid single working days between days off | Disruption of blocks of leisure time ↓ |

M = morning shift; E = evening shift; N = night shift; – = day off
*Source:* Knauth and Hornberger (2003) *Preventative and Compensatory Measures for Shift Workers.* By permission of Oxford University Press.

when developing a shift system. Although this book is primarily about night work, because night work is often embedded into a shift system that involves day shifts, it is worth considering the recommendations from Knauth and Hornberger (2003, p.110) regarding the sequencing of shifts, particularly night shifts (Table 3.1).

It is difficult with a small workforce to develop shift systems that suit everyone, but given the findings in relation to health cited earlier, it is critical that managers take account of the information in Table 3.1.

## Things managers and night workers need to address whilst they are on duty

### CASE STUDY 5: THE UBIQUITOUS CARDIGAN*

The night staff at the Gables Care Home were unable to tell us whose cardigan it was that was always around at night. They said it had been there for ages. It was a large, comfy item, with no particular attractiveness except its commodious and warming qualities.

Most of the staff used it at various times to warm themselves, particularly in the small hours in the middle of the night.

Relying on a cardigan is not enough. Other things need to be in place. The night-time cardigan is used because staff become cold in the middle of the night. Our bodies are programmed to be least efficient between 3 o'clock and 6 o'clock at night. This is when, if we are awake, we feel cold and tired and in need of warming comfort. It is also when we need the right type of food and drink.

---

*      With thanks to Kim McDougall of North Lanarkshire Council for raising my awareness of this phenomenon. I now see the cardigan everywhere.

## Night-time nutrition

Night-time nutrition is important to the maintenance of good health and wakefulness amongst staff. It is of concern, therefore, that in many care homes the kitchen is locked at night (this has consequences for residents as well as staff – an issue dealt with more fully in Chapter 7) or that staff are not allowed food on duty. If staff cannot access proper food, then they will resort to chocolate bars and 'quick fixes' to stave off hunger and give an energy boost.

During night shifts a main meal break should be taken between midnight and 1 a.m. with a shorter break between 3 a.m. and 4 a.m. (Wedderburn 1991). It has also been found that alertness during the night is improved after a meal consisting of protein rather than carbohydrate. If the kitchen is not fully open, then at least a microwave should be provided so that hot food can be produced. Bars of chocolate should be avoided: although they give a quick energy boost, this will be followed by sudden drop in energy levels.

How food is made available for staff is an important issue. It is better that staff have access to healthy snacks. A vending machine could provide snacks: Schwerha (2005) recommends that vending machines provide fruit, low-fat dairy and wholegrain food. The disadvantage of this type of provision is that it gives the unfortunate impression that staff are expected to pay for their own food. It is also worth pointing out here that vending machines can be noisy. The clunk of things dropping into the bottom needs to be considered when placing the machine.

Heavy, greasy or spicy food should be avoided. Such foods are difficult to digest at any time, but during the night when the disruption to the circadian rhythm impairs digestion they become even more problematic and can cause digestive problems. Workers should also be aware of their caffeine intake. Two or three cups of coffee during the first half of the shift will facilitate alertness. Coffee taken during the second half of the shift will impede workers' ability to sleep when they get home. It is much better to drink fruit juice as the night progresses.

## Napping

Generally 'sleeping on the job' is, at the very least, discouraged and often regarded as serious misconduct. However, sleep debt increases with each concurrent night shift, and fatigue accumulates with a resultant decrease in performance and an increase in health risks.

There is evidence, however, that the need to nap should be acknowledged and strategies developed to enable staff to undertake structured, permitted short naps. Managers need to weigh up the pros and cons of allowing or even supporting this practice. It appears to be the case that taking a nap during the night can increase vigilance and alertness (Dinges *et al.* 1987; Muzet *et al.* 1995; Rosekind, Smith and Miller 1995; Tepas 2000). It can be an effective strategy to decrease fatigue and improve performance. Bonneford *et al.* (2001) found that a short nap improved satisfaction with the quality and easiness of night work.

There is, however, evidence of a small negative effect of napping. This is what is often refereed to as 'sleep inertia' which occurs when the period after the nap leaves the person feeling less alert and slower to respond. This, however, is only a short-term effect, usually of around five minutes and at most 15 minutes (Kogi 2000).

If nap breaks are going to be instigated, then, of course, this needs to be organised effectively and should not detract from the care given to residents.

Kogi (2000, p.35) gives five rules of thumb that managers need to be aware of when organising napping for night workers:

1. Facilitate napping at the workplace by encouraging it.

2. Secure 60–90 minutes as a napping period where possible.

3. Select adequate temporal placement of the nap so that workers can nap in turns during the midnight and early morning hours.

4. Provide a good sleeping environment in a quiet, dark and air-conditioned area.

5. Collectively plan the nap periods as part of multifaceted measures for improving the shift working conditions.

Kogi (2000) warns however that 'Whilst napping is a useful strategy, we should not regard it as a decisive means of alleviating the night workload and fatigue' (p.35).

## Light levels

There is adequate evidence that night shift workers can improve nocturnal alertness and daytime sleep by bright light exposure whilst they are at work (Rimmer *et al.* 2000; Yoon *et al.* 2002). Light has great influence on the setting of our circadian rhythm. The use of blue light, present in sunlight, halogen and fluorescent lighting, is the most influential. McNair *et al.* (2010) recommend that night staff have a level of light exposure at night that is twice the normal level of a well-lit room. Although exposure to this light may well be useful at night, it will be counterproductive in the mornings during the last hours of the shift and after the shift is over. This, of course, is a time when staff may well be exposed to sunlight, and for this reason workers need to wear dark glasses on their way home so that they avoid natural sunlight which will waken them and reduce their chances of sleeping (Rimmer *et al.* 2000; Yoon *et al.* 2002). This is a complicated area and it may well be that some people do not benefit from bright light exposure. Iskra-Golec *et al.* (2000) found that the use of bright light led to a lowering of morale and motivation amongst some people. It is probably enough here to recommend that staff consider using bright light at periods throughout the night and work out for themselves if and how it affects them.

## Medical screening and support for night workers

As a member of the European Union (EU), the UK must abide by European law, which is legislated in part through the use of European directives. In the private sector these directives are not instantly applicable across Europe, but rather each member country of the EU is given some scope for national interpretation of the directive and a time limit is set for each member country to ensure its laws are made compatible. The directives are immediately enforceable in public bodies such as parliament, local authorities or hospitals.

There are several European directives which set out the requirements for working conditions within the EU. The European Working Time Directive (93/104/EC) (EWTD) addresses issues of night work and was implemented by the British parliament through the Working Time Regulations (1998) (WTR) which came into force on 1 October 1998.

The WTR contain special provisions for night workers which limit their hours and require employers to offer regular health assessments. The WTR states the following:

- Night workers should not work more than an average of eight hours in every 24.

- Night work is defined as a seven-hour period, which includes the period between midnight and 5 a.m. (usually 11 p.m. to 6 a.m.).

- Anyone who normally works at least three hours of their working day during this night period is classed as a night worker.

- Where such work involves any 'special hazards or heavy physical or mental strain' the eight-hours limit applies to each 24-hour period, not simply an average of eight hours over the reference period.

## Definition of a night worker

Although this was covered in Chapter 2, it is pertinent to repeat it here. Night workers are classed as those people who work for at least three hours of their shift as a normal course during 'night-time'. The definition of 'normal course' may be given a rather loose interpretation due to the case of R v Attorney General for Northern Ireland *ex parte* Burns (1999, IRLR 315) which held that the directive was not limited to those who only or mainly worked night shifts, but rather applied as long as working night shifts was a regular feature of the employment.

## Definition of night-time

Night-time is a defined term in the WTR as a period lasting not less than seven hours and which includes between midnight and 5 a.m. The default period for night-time under the WTR is 11 p.m. until 6 a.m. but this may be changed by a collective or workforce agreement to include such times as 10 p.m. to 5 a.m. or midnight to 7 a.m. or any time in between these two bands.

## Night work limits

The WTR sets out time limits on how long a night worker may work for. A night worker may not work for more than an average of eight hours for each 24 hours within a given 'reference period' (usually 17 weeks).

This is calculated by the use of a statutory formula: A / (B–C) where:

> **A** is the number of hours during the reference period which are normal working hours for that worker
>
> **B** is the number of days during the reference period, and
> **C** is the total number of hours during the reference period of rest time to which the worker is entitled.

The maximum time a night worker can work per week is 48 hours. This is because the calculation assumes that the total hours were performed over the permissible six days. There is, however, a more stringent protection in place for those night workers whose work involves special hazards or heavy physical or mental strain (Working Time Regulations 1998). Such workers may never work for more than eight hours in any 24-hour period; this is not an average calculation but rather a de facto eight-hour period.

It is not possible for individual workers to opt out of the night-time work limits. However, if a collective or workforce agreement is in force, then this may modify or even totally exclude the time limits. If any such agreement is in force, then it is binding on all workers, irrelevant of the fact of whether or not they are members of the union.

## Health assessments

Regulation 7 of the WTR has adopted both the wording of the International Labour Organisation's General Conference of 1990 and the EWTD. The union Amicus (2003) gives a helpful explanation:

> Workers assigned to night work should be offered a health assessment beforehand to determine their suitability for night work. An earlier health assessment may count. Once night work has commenced, regular health assessments should be offered.

The UK Government website www.direct.gov.uk expands on this and gives the following guidance on the subject of health care for night workers:

> As there are health risks linked with night work, your employer must offer you a free health assessment (normally a questionnaire) before you start working at night and on a regular basis after that. Generally this is done once a year, but your employers could offer a health assessment more frequently. You do not have to take the health check offered.

Your employer should get help from a suitably qualified health professional when devising and assessing the health assessments. If you do complete a health assessment questionnaire and the answers cause concern, your employer should refer you to a doctor. If a doctor tells you that you have health problems caused by night work, your employer must transfer you to daytime work – if this is possible.

It is not the remit of this book to detail all the regulations but to alert the reader to their existence and relevance. Further guidance on the working time regulations in relation to night work can be found on www.direct.gov.uk/en/Employment/Employees/WorkingHoursAndTimeOff/DG_10028519.

## Things night workers need to put in place for themselves after work

There are a number of strategies that night-shift workers can develop that should help them to get better sleep and so counteract some of the negative consequences of working at night. Problems cited above concerning concentration on the journey home should be tackled. A number of authors have suggested the following measures. It is probably significant for many employers and employees that some of these are unlikely to be implemented; others however, are simply common sense and are achievable.

- taking a nap before going home
- employer to provide a car pool
- keep the interior of the car cool
- listen to talk or music
- vary the route a bit
- use public transport
- move closer to the place of work.

(Adapted from Knauth and Hornberger 2003)

Once home, workers need to try to maximise their sleep. The following list of strategies and activities are suggestions that night staff should consider and which should help them to deal with the problems that they, as night workers, can face in establishing routines that aid sleep and help counteract the disruption to the circadian rhythm.

- Try to get seven to eight hours sleep at one time (National Sleep Foundation 2002).
- Try to establish a regular sleep routine.
- If you don't get to sleep within 15 minutes of going to bed, get up and try again later (Bootzin and Perils 1992).
- Try to go to bed at the same time after every night shift.
- Establish a regular wake-up time (Szuba, Kloss and Dinges 2003).
- Wear dark glasses when driving home (Burgess, Maguire and O'Keefe 2002).
- Seek exposure to bright light (sunlight is best) as soon as possible after waking (Burgess *et al.* 2002).
- Before going on to night shift try to get a quick 30–40 minutes' sleep before leaving home (Garbarino *et al.* 2004).
- Try to keep the bedroom at 65–70°F.
- Use blackout curtains in the bedroom whilst sleeping during the day.
- Make sure that clocks and other electrical equipment that glows are either turned off or covered.
- Reduce all potentially disturbing noises in the bedroom (e.g. telephone, clock noises, pets).
- Wear earplugs.
- Select a relaxation method to use within an hour of going to bed (e.g. deep breathing, warm bath or shower, reading).

- Avoid food, alcohol and drinks that are high in caffeine at least six hours before going to bed (Morin and Espie 2003).
- Avoid eating a heavy meal three to four hours before going to bed; eat the biggest meal of the day after waking.
- Eat high-protein, light meals while at work and before going to bed.
- Limit fluid intake to 8oz just before going to bed.
- If you awaken during the day, get up to use the bathroom, and, if hungry, eat a light protein snack in a dim or dark environment, then return to bed.
- Discuss with your GP any remedies, non-pharmaceutical as well as pharmaceutical, that might help you sleep.
- Try to get half an hour's exercise at least three times a week.
- Don't do demanding exercises during the three hours before you go to bed.
- Hang a sign on the bedroom door noting 'day sleeper' as a reminder to family.
- Discuss individual needs for sleep with family and friends.
- Choose social activities wisely (i.e. avoid activities at the time sleep typically is scheduled).

*Source*: 'Impact of shift work on the health and safety of nurses and patients' by A.M. Berger and B.B. Hobbs in *Clinical Journal of Oncology Nursing 10*, p.468. Copyright 2006 by the Oncology Nursing Society. Adapted with permission.

It might not be practical or indeed desirable to implement all of the above suggestions. It might be better to identify some key areas and concentrate on those initially. With this in mind Shapiro *et al.* (1997) developed the following excellent checklist for shift workers. It enables individuals to identify up to three specific areas that they need to and could improve on relatively easily.

# Sleep hygiene chart
## (Circle the response that applies to you.)

| | Good | Bad |
|---|---|---|
| Do you wake at the same time each day? | YES | NO |
| Do you exercise each day? | YES | NO |
| Do you set aside time daily to deal with stress (e.g. to list next day's tasks)? | YES | NO |
| Do you have time to unwind before bedtime? | YES | NO |
| Do you have regular behaviours before bedtime? | YES | NO |
| Do you have a hot shower or bath before bed? | YES | NO |
| Do you go to bed when drowsy? | YES | NO |
| Is your bed comfortable? | YES | NO |
| Is your bedroom secure? | YES | NO |
| Is your bedroom quiet, cool and dark? | YES | NO |
| Do you exercise close to bedtime? | NO | YES |
| Do you have any caffeine less than five hours before you go to sleep? | NO | YES |
| Do you smoke less than three hours before bed? | NO | YES |
| Do you have much to eat within the two hours before going to bed? | NO | YES |
| Do you consume much fluid within the two hours before going to bed? | NO | YES |
| Do you drink alcohol within two hours before going to bed? | NO | YES |
| Do you occasionally nap in the day? | NO | YES |
| Do you take non-prescription drugs? | NO | YES |

Select two or three items in the bad column and try to change those behaviours. Again don't be too rigid with this – don't punish yourself but try to identify some achievable goals.

## Summary

This chapter has highlighted many of the health risks involved in working at night. It has also identified ways of minimising the potentially negative health effects. We do not intend to discourage people from working at nights, but rather to ensure that people are made aware of and are well informed about the implications of doing night work.

Health problems are not an automatic result of working nights; however, there is evidence that working exclusively at nights or as part of a shift system can damage health (Costa and Pokorski 2000; International Agency for Research on Cancer 2007; Knutsson 2003).There are many reasons for this, but the fact that people are working against their natural circadian rhythm is a major factor.

Managers can ensure that night staff are given the best possible information and support to enable them to continue to work in a healthy way. This can include using different shift patterns, ensuring that staff have access to healthy food, providing exposure to bright light and following the European Working Time Directive (93/104/EC) which contains special provisions for night workers.

# Chapter 4

# Understanding Dementia: What Night Staff Need to Know and Do

A high proportion of people in care homes have some form of dementia, with recent estimates claiming 62 per cent of residents have dementia (Matthews and Denning 2002); and in the UK over half of all people with dementia are thought to live in a care home (MacDonald and Carpenter 2003). If night staff are going to give support and care that is based on sound evidence-based interventions, then it is essential that they have a good understanding of the way people are affected by dementia and the consequent needs that have to be met.

## CASE STUDY 6

Valerie was an 80-year-old woman. She had been widowed for three years. Her two children lived abroad and visited once a year.

Valerie had always been a fiercely independent woman. She worked for most of her life in the local hospital where she was a ward sister. She was rightly proud of her nursing skills and the status that this gave her. She worked for many years as a night sister on a surgical ward. Since the death of her husband she had lived alone. She had a number of interests and hobbies. She was a member of the local book group; she walked with a ramblers group and helped out at a charity shop locally; she was physically very fit.

Valerie's behaviour started to cause concern amongst her neighbours and friends. She had been found walking about the local streets at 11 o'clock at night. When asked what she was doing, she became angry and shouted that she had missed the bus and people should mind their own business. Her next door neighbours often heard much noise throughout the night coming from Valerie's house. They wondered if she was sleeping at all at night.

Valerie also started to behave strangely when she was working at the charity shop. She became easily confused, lost things and became agitated about apparently trivial things. She had also started to talk at length to customers, telling stories about her time on the wards, as though they were recent events.

Valerie had dementia.

## What is dementia?

Dementia is an umbrella term used to describe a wide variety of diseases and disorders of the brain. It is a syndrome characterised by a decline in cognitive function and memory from previously attained intellectual levels, which is sustained over a period of months or years. The deterioration is of such severity that it impairs the affected individual's ability to work and to perform activities of daily living, including communication (Molloy and Lubiniski 1995).

Any definition and attempt to understand dementia needs to take account of the experience of the person with the condition. Although the above definition is accurate in its description of the way in which the condition affects people physically, it does not take account of the other profound implications: psychological, emotional and social.

The following definition by Cheston and Bender (1999, p.147) gives a clear insight into the meaning of the condition for the person with dementia.

> The experience of dementia is characterised by both the experience of loss (of social roles and relationship as well as of neurological functioning) and the threat of further losses to come and results in a range of emotions including grief, depression, anxiety, despair and terror. The experience of dementia therefore represents a profound threat to the individual's identity…to their sense of who they are.

Dementia affects about 1.4 per cent of people aged 65–69, 2.8 per cent of people aged 70–74, 5.6 per cent of people aged 75–79, 10.5 per cent of people aged 80–84, 20.8 per cent of people aged 85–89 and 38.6 per cent of people aged 90–95 (Jorm and Jolley 1998). There are 820,000 people living with dementia in the UK today, a number forecast to rise rapidly as the population ages (Alzheimer's Research Trust 2010). Because people are living longer, there is an increasing number of people living with dementia. There are many different types of dementia and people will be affected differently depending on the type of dementia they have.

The most frequently experienced dementias are:

- Alzheimer's type dementia
- vascular or multi-infarct dementia
- dementia of Lewy body type
- frontal lobe dementia
- Pick's disease
- Parkinson's disease dementia
- Huntington's disease dementia
- alcohol-related dementia (Korsakoff's)
- AIDS-related dementia.

It is not necessary, for the purposes of this book, to describe all these dementias. The most common are described briefly below in Table 4.1.

## Table 4.1 Common forms of dementia

| | |
|---|---|
| **Alzheimer's type dementia** | Accounts for around 55% of patients diagnosed with dementia (Killeen 2000).<br><br>A degenerative disease affecting the brain. Changes caused by the production of plaques containing a protein called beta-amyloid protein and neurofibrillary tangles which form in areas of brain tissue and destroy them. The temporal and parietal lobes of the brain are generally affected, which can result in significant memory loss and an inability to recognise people and places. It can be extremely distressing, particularly if a person no longer recognises her image or friends and family (Kitwood 1997).<br><br>With progression, basic skills and capabilities are lost. Visual-spatial skills can become impaired, resulting in patient becoming unable to put sequences of activity or movement together, e.g. placing her arm into her clothing (Jenkins 1998). The frontal lobe can also be affected, resulting in difficulties in communication and judgement and disinhibited behaviour (Jacques and Jackson 2000). Symptoms progress gradually but persistently over time (Burns, Howard and Pettit 1997). |
| **Lewy body type** | Lewy bodies are tiny spots containing deposits of a protein called alpha-synuclein. They are found in the hippocampus, temporal lobe and neocortex, in addition to the classic sites in the substantia nigra and other subcortical regions (Del Ser *et al.* 2000). Patients with Parkinson's disease also have Lewy bodies, but it is the higher density of these in Lewy body dementia that differentiates between the two conditions (McKeith *et al.* 1995).<br><br>Lewy body dementia often results in fluctuations in cognitive impairment, which lead to episodic confusion and lucid intervals. These fluctuations in cognition can occur over minutes, hours or days. They can occur in as many as 50–70% of patients and are associated with shifting levels of attention and alertness (Archibald 2003).<br><br>Patients with Lewy body dementia can experience visual and auditory hallucinations, secondary delusions and falls. These symptoms can result in the person presenting with behaviours that are challenging. Treatment plans, therefore, may include consideration of the use of neuroleptic (antipsychotic) medication. However, there needs to be extreme caution in the use of antipsychotic medication as people with Lewy body dementia have neuroleptic sensitivity (McKeith *et al.* 1992; Aarsland *et al.* 2005). Other side effects include sedation, immobility, rigidity, postural instability, falls and increased confusion. Dehydration, another feature of this disease, is often associated with poor outcomes such as increased mortality rates (Barber, Pannikar and McKeith 2001); therefore, a greater awareness of this form of dementia is important.<br><br>Lewy body dementia is the third most prevalent type of dementia, accounting for approximately 20% of people with dementia (McKeith *et al.* 1995). Del Ser *et al.* (2000) suggest that the figure may be closer to 36%. |

### Table 4.1 Common forms of dementia *cont.*

| | |
|---|---|
| **Vascular dementia** | Also referred to as multi-infarct dementia. Caused by problems in the circulation of blood to the brain, resulting in multiple strokes to brain tissue and significant cognitive impairment (Sander 2002). These strokes can result in damage to areas of the brain responsible for speech or language and produce generalised symptoms of dementia. As a result, vascular dementia may appear similar to Alzheimer's type dementia.<br><br>Vascular dementia can progress in an irregular manner with episodes of sudden loss. Can also take the pattern of gradual change, as in Alzheimer's type dementia. The rate of memory loss and insight associated with vascular dementia appears to progress at a slower rate than in Alzheimer type dementia.<br><br>Vascular dementia is identified as distinct condition in up to 20% of people with dementia (Miller and Morris 1993); however, as with all types of dementia it can co-exist with other forms of the condition. It is considered the second most common form of dementia in the Western world (Nor, McIntosh and Jackson 2005). |

Table 4.1 gives a short description of the commonest forms of dementia. It is important to emphasise, however, that even when people have the same type of dementia, they can experience it differently and can present different symptoms, characteristics and behaviours. The impact of the condition on people will be determined by their previous health experiences, their personality, the existence of any other disability, their social and cultural history and their coping mechanisms.

Additionally, although the damage is irreversible, it is characteristic of people with dementia to be more receptive some days than others and even to change throughout the course of the day. This may be in part due to an on–off impulse in the transmission of signals in the cells or because the person has fewer resources to call on, and so is much more likely to be affected by things such as tiredness, stress, anxiety and physical illness.

## The brain and its functions

The progression of the condition into different areas of the brain will impair and destroy the function of that part of the brain. It is not essential to have a detailed knowledge of the brain to understand the person with dementia. It can be useful, however, to know how the different functions are grouped. This helps in the understanding of specific behaviours and, more importantly, in the understanding of paradoxical behaviours that often appear. It also helps in making decisions about which skills and behaviours are to be encouraged and maintained and which are lost to function for ever. Figure 4.1 gives a basic introduction to the different parts of the brain, their functions and which behaviours they stimulate or control.

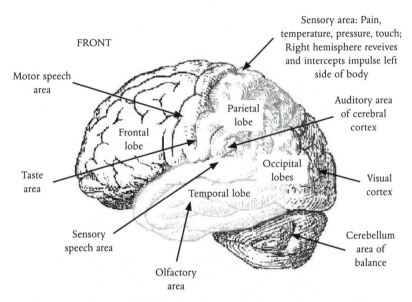

Figure 4.1 Side view of the brain (Dementia Services Development Centre, University of Stirling 1997)

## Temporal lobes

These are located on either side of the brain. The left or dominant lobe (in people who are right-handed) stores verbal memory. The right-side lobe stores visual memory. Smell and taste are located on both sides. These lobes are involved in our ability to learn new things. Recent memory is laid, recorded and stored and is then moved back and stored deep inside the temporal lobes. With the onset of dementia, damage occurs to the lobes and recent memory is lost. Frequently used and strongly stored memories will remain for some time, but as the disease progresses these too will be lost.

## Parietal lobes

These are also located on either side of the brain, with each side having a specific function. The left side is the analytical and logical centre and is the area that controls patterning. It is therefore important in our use of language, which involves the patterning of words, in our ability to do arithmetic and hence manage money, and in our understanding of the pattern or geography of our body. This lobe tells us which is our right side and which our left, critical information when dressing. When this lobe is damaged, people will have difficulty constructing sentences and with reading and writing. They will also have difficulty with dressing. This is important for carers to know, because once the ability to remember patterns has gone, no amount of explaining or showing will get the patterns back. There will come a point, for example, when the person can no longer dress himself. However, it may be that the person can remember two patterns but not three, so one needs to be cautious in deciding when all function has gone.

The right-side lobe is our three-dimensional centre. This tells us where we are in space and helps us to get around our environment. Once this is damaged, people will have difficulty in locating themselves and in making sense of their surroundings. In particular, they will have difficulty in seeing changes of levels and will often misinterpret changes in texture and colour, seeing steps where there are none and not seeing those that are there.

## Frontal lobes

These are where new learning takes place before being passed back into the parietal lobes. This is our planning and organising centre. Important in understanding some behaviour seen in Alzheimer's disease, it is also where our 'initiator' is. This is the part that gets us going to do things. When this is damaged, people may sit and do nothing, not because they cannot do anything but because their initiator cannot get them going. If someone else takes the role of initiator, then the person will engage in activity. One problem, however, is that once the person has started to do something, the initiator does not switch off automatically and they may continue to do the same thing over and over again (perseveration) until prompted into doing something else. These lobes are also where we store our knowledge of socially appropriate behaviour.

## Limbic region

This controls sleep, appetite and emotions. It can be disrupted when the frontal and temporal lobes are affected.

## Cerebellum

This controls balance and the coordination of voluntary movements such as walking and sitting.

## Hypothalamus

The hypothalamus works to produce homeostasis, a state of equilibrium. It regulates the body's metabolism. It is the part of the brain that controls hunger, thirst and body temperature. It influences food intake, weight regulation, fluid intake and balance, thirst, body heat and the sleep cycle. The hypothalamus also controls the action of the pituitary gland.

Functions are not necessarily restricted to one area of the brain. This can help to explain why people will sometimes retain some functions even when the primary site for that function is damaged. Those functions that are related to memory, for example, are located in a number of areas.

# Working with different realities

To understand the difficulties that people with dementia experience in relation to their memory and understanding of where they are, what they are doing and who they and others are, it is necessary to understand some of the ways in which memory is stored and subsequently damaged by the dementia.

We have two kinds of memory – short-term and long-term memory. New information is stored in our short-term memory for about 20–30 seconds before being transported into our long-term memory. This is not an automatic process. Whether we retain information by moving it back into our long-term memory depends on the way the information is given, received and experienced. It also requires us to work at it. We need to pay attention and concentrate. Other influencing factors are the emotional content of the information or event. The more emotionally significant, the more likely it is to become embedded in our memory. Repetition of information, events and skills will aid retention, and seeing information or being able to visualise it significantly aids the storing of information. The use of association is also important. We can remember something if we can 'hang' the information on to something else that we can associate it with, and, of course, the more meaningful the information, the more chance there is that it will be retained in our memory.

When someone develops dementia, even if the above conditions apply, the ability to retain the memory and move it back into the long-term memory becomes increasingly disturbed and eventually lost. From the time of the onset of the dementia, therefore, the amount of new information stored will be diminished.

As the dementia progresses, even information and events that are stored in the long-term memory will begin to disappear. Huub Buijssen (2005) describes and illustrates this process through the idea of diaries. He describes our memory as stored in diaries, one for each year of our life. People without dementia will have all their diaries stored chronologically and intact on the shelf.

If we imagine a shelf of diaries, one diary for each year of our life, then with the onset of dementia memories begin to get lost and a domino effect takes place with the diaries slowly falling down. Only those left standing will have meaning and memory for the person. Buijssen describes this as rollback memory (see Figure 4.2).

The memory of a 77-year-old without dementia – the shelf on which the diaries containing the memories of his entire life are stacked is still intact.

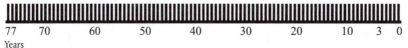

77    70       60        50        40        30        20        10    3    0
Years

The memory of a 77-year-old patient with dementia who has lost his memories of the last 17 years – the diaries begin to collapse, first the most recent, then those preceeding them, and so on.

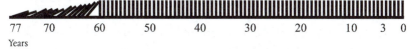

77    70       60        50        40        30        20        10    3    0
Years

The memory of someone in the advanced stage of dementia – only the memories of his early childhood remain.

77    70       60        50        40        30        20        10    3    0
Years

Figure 4.2 The roll-back memory (Buijssen 2005)

When the part of the brain that has short-term and recent memory is damaged, the person will make sense of the information and stimuli in that part of the brain that is functioning. As illustrated by Buijssen's diaries in Figure 4.2, this will be the part that has memory from further and further back. New information will be made sense of within the diaries that remain. The person's sense of reality will not be in the here and now, in our reality, but the there and then, her past.

## CASE STUDY 7: DIANA KERR

I often illustrate this point in relation to my own possible reactions to developing dementia and being moved to live in a home for older people in later life. Part of my job is to visit homes for older people and to train staff. This means that I am often in homes for older people where the staff are sitting around, listening attentively with occasional discussion and conversation.

If I develop dementia in later life and find myself in a home for older people, I will make sense of my environment in relation to my past rather than the then present. To be in a home where people are sitting around often not speaking will present a well-known and well-understood scenario. I will believe that I am there to train the staff. The long-term memory part of my brain will interpret all the immediate information and stimuli, making sense of them in my long-term memory, and this will confirm that I am the teacher and certainly not a resident. What, of course, is almost unbearable is the realisation that as a teacher I would reasonably expect to go home at the end of the afternoon. To be told that 'this is your home now' would be both incredible and terrifying.

People with dementia are making sense of the world around them using the brain that is functioning, which increasingly is the long-term rather than the short-term memory. This means that often they perceive and understand the world from a different time and place and therefore will have a different reality. This difference can be and often is a source of immense anxiety and fear for people with dementia. The following exercise illustrates this point well.

---

Imagine you set off from your house to your local pub to meet your friends. You always go as soon as your favourite soap on the television is over; in fact, the tune at the end is the signal for you to put your coat on.

On the way there, two people come up to you and take you by the arm and refuse to let you go on any further. They insist on you going with them.

Imagine what you might feel. What might you think was going on? What might you do and say? It is not hard to imagine the panic and fear that this might engender.

---

Because the brain is damaged and cognitive skills diminished, the 'trigger' of the music results in the person re-enacting past behaviours and realities. People from the present become unrecognisable. They did not exist in the past.

The dementia means that people begin to lose the ability to recognise the familiar. They will see the world as a foreign place peopled by strangers (Meisen 1993). This can happen even when they remain at home surrounded by people they have known for many years and who are caring and supportive of them. It is not just a consequence of being moved into different settings such as hospitals or residential or nursing homes.

Of course, the desire to be in the past may also be psychologically functional. If the present is full of fear, anxiety and an assault on the sense of self, it may be safer to be in the past. It is important not to see the 'not being in the here and now' as simply a function of the changes in the brain, but to recognise this as a complex dynamic between the physical, social and psychological changes and the needs of the person with dementia.

This is well illustrated by the following case study of Valerie, who, after receiving a diagnosis of dementia, went to live in a care home for older people.

### CASE STUDY 8

Valerie moved to the Elms Care Home soon after she received a diagnosis of dementia. She spent most of the day walking around the house, in what might have appeared to be 'wandering' behaviour. This was, however, clearly a purposeful activity for Valerie who walked with gusto and often gave orders to staff as she passed them. She would also try to get some residents out of their chairs and insist they 'follow me'.

At night Valerie was particularly agitated. She would refuse to go to bed during the evening, and once in bed, as often as not, she would get up, get dressed, after a fashion, and start to walk around the house. She would go into people's bedrooms and 'check them'. She would call the staff and tell them to go into 'so and so's' room, demand the medicine trolley and sometimes, in an agitated state, rush about 'looking for a doctor'.

The staff reported that her 'wandering' behaviour was a problem. They would take her back to bed whenever she got up. But this had very little effect as she soon re-emerged from her room, often in an even more agitated state. The staff asked for some sort of sedation to be prescribed to help her sleep.

Few of the night staff knew Valerie's life story; agency and bank staff, who often worked at night, knew nothing of her past.

### What did night staff need to know and do to support Valerie?

It can be seen from this case study that Valerie's behaviour was not being understood and that, as a consequence, inappropriate and potentially harmful interventions were being put in place.

### What did staff need to know to give Valerie the right support?

If the staff had known more about how dementia affects people's reality, they would then have recognised that her behaviour may have been a reactivated past behaviour. They needed to know her life story so that they could make sense of her reality, which was now back in the days when she was at work.

They should have known about her career as a night nurse. This would have helped staff to understand that Valerie's reality was back to the time when she had to go to work at night. Clearly she believed that she was again working on the wards and so needed to walk about checking on things and people.

What seemed like 'wandering' behaviour was clearly a purposeful, necessary and satisfying activity for Valerie.

## What could staff have done to help her?

It would have been stress-reducing if staff had been proactive in enabling Valerie to carry out her perceived night duties. It might have helped if she had been invited to sit with the nurses, to have been given some paper work or asked to accompany them on their rounds. It was certainly not helpful to try to get her straight back to bed.

A suggestion that it was time for a tea break would have taken Valerie's mind off the work. She then might have been able to go 'home' to bed. A useful response to her agitation might have been to say, 'Valerie, you are not on duty tonight, but let's have a cup of tea before you go to bed.'

All her working life Valerie had slept in the day and worked at night. It would be helpful to make sure that the environment was as conducive to sleep as possible, and to check that noise or lights were not waking Valerie. Once she woke she thought she had to go to work.

This case study illustrates a number of important actions and principles when supporting people with dementia at night:

- Try to go with the flow.
- Do not confront or contradict.
- Recognise the person's reality and needs.
- Check that the environment is not causing the problem behaviour.

Core to working with people with dementia is to recognise that if you do not know their past, then you cannot understand their present. Life-story work is key to this.

It may well be that daytime staff and/or activities coordinators have done life-story work with people, but often this is not available for night staff. It is equally important that night staff have access to this work. Chapter 9 will cover life-story work and how night staff can use it appropriately.

Night staff need the same levels of training on dementia as day staff. It is a fallacy that people with dementia are asleep at night. People with dementia, partly because of changes to their circadian rhythm, wake at night. Staff need to help them return to sleep where this is possible, but staff also need to be aware that when people wake they often need comfort and company. People with dementia additionally may well be disorientated and forget where they are, what they are doing, how old they are and who staff are. Staff need to respond to this by entering the person's reality and world and not confronting them.

## CASE STUDY 9

Angus moved into a care home not long after his diagnosis of dementia. Initially he went to bed at around 10 o'clock and slept through the night, or at least if he woke, he soon went back to sleep again.

One evening at about 7 o'clock the staff found him outside the home wandering about. When the staff told him to come in, he became uncharacteristically angry. The following night he was lost. The police brought him back. The next night as he went to leave, the staff forbade him, telling him he was to stay in and go to bed. He became very angry and hit out.

The staff reported that he was now 'aggressive' as well as 'wandering'. The night staff asked for some sedation to calm him at night when he became increasingly agitated and angry. He would shout and swear that he would get them the sack if they kept interfering. A few nights later he was again lost, but the home received a phone call from a large, well-known hotel in the city. Angus had turned up 'for his night shift'.

Angus had been a night porter at the hotel for many years before his retirement. He was now back in the diaries for those years, and when everyone in the home got ready for bed and as the dark fell, he set off for work. Clearly the staff response so far had caused him frustration, grief and anger. Orientating him to reality was not what was needed. After some discussion it was decided that as the night fell the staff would put pairs of shoes outside each bedroom. Angus soon saw this as his night-time job; this was one of his tasks at the hotel (of course, the home itself had sufficient resemblances to a hotel to satisfy Angus's need to do his job).

After the shoes were cleaned the staff would thank him for a good nights work and suggest he now get his sleep.

This is a good example of the need to go with the flow. The initial staff response was to label Angus's behaviour as 'wandering' and 'aggressive'. These are two 'challenging behaviours' often attributed to people with dementia. What the staff were doing was misunderstanding Angus's behaviour and what he was attempting to do. Cheston and Bender (1999, p.47) address this issue when they write:

> The adaptive response of people with dementia, the ways in which they attempt to cope with dementia, are often misinterpreted as further evidence of impairment.

> Consequently, these behavioural strategies and emotional reactions are often seen not as responses of people to a ghastly predicament but as proof of a degenerative process occurring within the brain.

The initial response of using reality orientation missed the need to see how Angus was coping and making sense of his world. It only served to push him into what was seen as challenging behaviour. The staff were not entering his reality nor were they responding to his worries, anxieties and needs.

In the second response known as 'validation', the staff reinforced Angus's identity: they validated Angus as a person. They recognised his need to do his job and they accepted his worries about not doing it properly. They set up an activity which engaged him, reduced his anxiety and, importantly, also got him over the triggers of nightfall and people going to bed, which acted as a reminder that he needed to get off for work.

Night staff working with people with dementia must know about the ways in which people with dementia try to cope, their different realities and their life history. Without this knowledge there is a danger that staff will continue to respond in ways that can be potentially distressing, inappropriate and harmful to people with dementia.

It is not the remit of this book to provide all the information on dementia that staff need. It is hoped that this chapter has highlighted some critical issues and will encourage staff to seek out training and further reading to fill in the gaps.

## Summary

Dementia is an umbrella term that covers many different conditions. Alzheimer's type dementia, vascular dementia and Lewy body dementia are the conditions most likely to be encountered by staff in care homes.

The experience of dementia can be frightening, anxiety-provoking, disorientating and can leave the person with an overwhelming sense of loss. It is important that staff have a good understanding of the ways in which people experience the condition if they are going to respond with understanding and not exacerbate the negative experiences.

The damage caused to the brain by the onset of dementia means that people begin to lose their short-term memory and will experience the world with the brain that is left intact; increasingly this will be their longer-term memories. Their reality will often be different to ours and increasingly it will be located in their past. It is critical, therefore, that staff understand people's past in order to understand their present behaviour, needs and emotions.

# Chapter 5

# Sleep, Ageing and Group Care

Night staff in residential and nursing homes usually see their primary task to be the promotion of sleep. It is important, therefore, that they have some understanding not only of the nature of normal sleep but also of what disturbs sleep and how to help people to sleep well.

### CASE STUDY 10

Sally was always a good sleeper. She stated, 'I went to sleep the minute my head hit the pillow' and 'I could sleep anywhere all night long'. Sally also stated that she rarely slept in the day; in fact, she found it hard to do so even if she thought she needed to if she had a busy night ahead.

Now in her late 60s, Sally tells of some distinct changes in her sleep patterns. She now reports having disturbed nights. She says she is now a 'light sleeper'. She wakes easily through the night, often three or four times. She also wakes earlier in the mornings. She has also started occasionally to have a nap after lunch – for Sally a previously unheard of, indeed scorned, activity.

Sally's story is a good illustration of a fairly common set of sleep changes noted by people as they get older. Up to 50 per cent of older people complain of sleep problems (Vitiello 2006) such as light sleep, frequent waking, early morning waking and undesired daytime sleep (Foley, Monjan and Brown 1995; Foley, Monjan and

Simonsick 1999; Vitiello, Foley and Stratton 2004). Older people also report that they take longer to fall asleep; they sleep fewer hours at night and wake earlier than they would like in the mornings (Foley *et al.* 1995). Moreover, older adults find that they are more sensitive to auditory stimuli so that noises in the environment are more likely to wake them. This is probably the consequence of an age-related lightening of sleep homeostatic processes (Dijk, Duffy and Reil 1999; Dijk, Duffy and Zeisler 2001).

The increase in night-time waking often leads to an increase in daytime fatigue, which will inevitably lead to an increase in daytime napping. Vitiello (2006) comments that this results in older people becoming 'larks' rather than 'owls'.

These changes in sleep levels and sleep duration are probably the consequence of changes to the circadian rhythm (the biological clock that tells our brains, and therefore our bodies, when it is day and night and so when it is time to sleep and to wake). This rhythm, which becomes more disturbed as people grow older, means that they are less able to compensate for any changes to sleep patterns caused by things such as jet lag or shift work.

Although some of these changes are part and parcel of growing older, they are not a bother to many older people. It is worth noting here that the above are general comments, and if 50 per cent of older people report problems with sleep, then there are 50 per cent who are not complaining. In fact, healthy older adults report fewer sleep problems than those with underlying health issues (Prinz *et al.* 1990).

It is important not to attribute all changes in sleep behaviour to simply growing older and to assume that it is an inevitability that must be endured. Certainly the sleep disorders associated with older age do seem to increase as people age, but these seem to generally happen slowly over many years (Vitiello 2006).

It is important that night staff have an understanding of both what is perhaps within the normal range of sleep variations and what is pathological. Staff are right to be concerned about sleep: getting a 'good night's sleep' is often a high priority for quality of life. Sleeping well is both an indicator and predictor of good health. One study (Manabe, Matsuit and Yanaya 2000) found that not sleeping at night led to an increased risk of shorter survival rates, even after adjustments for age, gender, diet and activities of daily living. Avidan *et al.* (2005) also found a possible link between insomnia and an increase in falls amongst elderly people in nursing homes. This was a small study and there is a need for more evidence. It would not be surprising, however, to find that tired and confused people are less stable on their feet and more likely to stumble.

## CASE STUDY 11

Jim didn't like to go to bed. He was often up well into the early hours, moving from lounge to hallway and back to lounge throughout the night. He didn't seem to want anything in particular, but he did like short conversations with staff. Many of the staff just accepted that he didn't want to sleep, although he looked very tired, with red eyes.

The care home introduced a system of key workers for the night staff and Jim's key worker, Alice, sat with him over a number of nights and asked why he didn't go to bed. Slowly Jim's story emerged: he felt very lonely and frightened during the night and was scared of dying. He had been married to Jean for 48 years, and when she died he found it very difficult to adjust to sleeping alone.

As he built up a relationship with Alice, she suggested that he might like to have a night light and he was willing to try this. He also asked if staff could sit with him sometimes and chat. Both these things helped and over a number of weeks Jim did start going to bed and managed to sleep for a few hours each night. He told Alice that he felt easier at nights now, although he still liked to stay up late.

This case study illustrates a number of issues that staff face when trying to help residents to maintain satisfactory sleep levels and sleep patterns.

As indicated above, many older people will experience irregular, interrupted and light sleep. What is important is that night staff respond appropriately to the person. In Jim's case there was an upsetting but clear cause of his sleep deprivation, and the staff responded appropriately and sensitively. The reasons are not always so clear; indeed, sometimes there may be no obvious cause. There are, however, a number of causes of poor sleep amongst older adults that are not the inevitable result of being older but are linked to the onset of certain conditions, both medical and psychological, and to the consequences of the use of certain medications (Bloom *et al.* 2009).

The following are possible causes of sleep disturbance:

- pain from acute conditions and illnesses such as toothache, earache, pulled muscles
- pain from chronic conditions such as arthritis
- chronic cardiac or pulmonary disease
- gastroesophageal reflux disorder
- depression
- neurological disorders such as Parkinson's disease and dementia
- the use of diuretics which increase need to urinate during the night
- stimulating agents (such as sympathomimetics, bronchodilators, antidepressants; antiparkinsonian agents, antihypertensives and cholinesterase inhibitors taken near bedtime
- sedating medications taken during the day which can contribute to daytime drowsiness and a disruption of the sleep–wake cycle
- inappropriate use of over-the-counter medication
- sleep-disordered breathing (sleep apnoea)
- restless leg syndrome
- rapid eye movement disorder

- lifestyle changes that reduce the need for regular bed and rise times
- low levels of exercise
- bereavement
- jet-lag
- daytime napping
- noise
- wrong temperature
- low exposure to daily sunlight
- high exposure to intermittent light at night
- bedding
- moving to a new home or smaller space
- moving to a retirement community or institutional care.

(Adapted from Fiorentino and Ancoli-Israel 2006)

This is a long list. No wonder older people have problems with sleep, particularly if they are in some form of group living in institutional care. As can be seen from the list, there are a number of things that make people in residential and nursing home care more vulnerable to sleep disturbance. Older people living in institutional type settings are known to be more susceptible to sleep disturbance than those living in the community. This is partly because a high proportion of people in such settings have dementia, but it is also because of other factors such as social isolation, low levels of activity, common sleeping rooms and extended time spent in bed (Fiorentino and Ancoli-Israel 2006).

Fiorentino and Ancoli-Israel (2006, p.294) report that 'sleep disturbance and daytime sleeping are rarely documented in medical records'. Yet it is essential that a proper assessment and diagnosis be carried out to determine if there are underlying health causes of the disturbed sleep. Sleep and sleep disorders can be assessed relatively simply. The starting point is to record a full medical examination and a medication history that includes over-the-counter and herbal products (Monane 1992). At this early stage of assessment it can usually be decided if the problem is transient, short-term or chronic (Schnieder 2002). More complex assessment can involve information on heart rate, blood pressure, respiration, body movements, etc. (Martin 2000). Polysomnography (PSG) is the process of recording all this information overnight. Wrist activity monitors that are portable now allow for effective polysomnography in the person's usual bed rather than having to have information recorded in a sleep laboratory.

Once medical and medication issues have been identified and rectified or ruled out as a cause of disturbance, staff need to consider environmental influences and practices that might be having a negative influence on night-time sleep. Exposure to bright light has been shown to be a major contributor to having a good sleep–wake cycle (Fiorentino and Ancoli-Israel 2006). Unfortunately, people living in care homes are exposed to very low levels of bright light. Ancoli-Israel, Parker and Sinaee (1997) and Schochat et al. (2000) have shown that the median daily light exposure for people with dementia living in nursing homes is only one minute of very bright light (more than 2500 lux) and 10.5 minutes of moderate bright light (more than 1000 lux). Four per cent of people in the studies were never exposed to bright light. Clearly this is an area that night staff do not have much control over, but managers need to take this into account when developing good sleep support regimes.

Night staff need to be constantly aware of noise levels which have a negative effect on people's ability to sleep soundly. Schnelle et al. (1993a, 1993b) found that there were 32 episodes of loud noise per night. Noise levels increased up to midnight, then decreased from 1–4 a.m. The source of the noise was mostly staff talking loudly or staff making noises with squeaking trolleys. A minority of time the noise was caused by residents (Kerr et al. 2008; Schnelle et al. 1993a, 1993b).

Another cause of sleep disturbance is intermittent light changes (Kerr et al. 2008). Schnelle et al. (1993a, 1993b) found that there were five light changes (lights being turned on and off) per night. In the study it was found that 50 per cent of awakenings of more than four minutes were the result of either noise or light. More is written about these issues in Chapters 6 and 8.

## Summary

The promotion of sleep during the night is an important aspect of the night staff role. It is essential, therefore, that night staff have some understanding not only of the nature of normal sleep but of what disturbs sleep and how to help people sleep well. The sleep patterns of people change as they get older. These changes in sleep levels and sleep duration are probably the consequence of changes to the circadian rhythm. Nevertheless, healthy older adults report fewer sleep problems than those with underlying health issues (Prinz *et al.* 1990). Many people in care homes will have health problems.

There are a number of possible causes of sleep disturbance such as pain, disease, depression, the need to go to the toilet, bereavement, noise, staff 'checking', changes in the environment or routine, insufficient daytime light, insufficient exercise and the effects of certain medications.

# Chapter 6

# Night-Time Checking

The issue of checking has been treated as a separate and specific area of practice because it highlights many of the issues that are dealt with in greater depth throughout the rest of the book. A central role of night staff is to ensure that residents are safe, that sleep is promoted as appropriate, and that people's medical, social and emotional needs are attended to. An important mechanism for meeting these needs is the use of discriminate, appropriate minimal checking.

Staff need to make sure that people are not left in saturated incontinence pads, that they are not distressed, that they are safe in bed and that they are receiving any night-time medical care and attention that they require. These requirements involve staff in maintaining oversight of all the residents. For some this will necessitate proactive checking which involves entering rooms; for others, minimal checking at the door of the room would suffice; and for others no checking will be required.

How and how often the checking is carried out depends on a number of variables such as the number and competence of staff, the use of agency staff, the extent of the use of technology such as alarm systems, the building design and the use of risk assessments.

The recognition that 'Older adults are more easily aroused from night-time sleep by auditory stimuli' (Vitiello 2006, p.171) means that opening a bedroom door, no matter how carefully done, or walking on creaky boards outside a bedroom whilst checking may be sufficient to cause someone to wake. For this reason and others discussed below, it is vital that staff are aware of the need to avoid excessive, indiscriminate checking.

In a study carried out by Kerr *et al.* (2008) it was found that night staff generally over-checked. Fear amongst night staff that someone will be found wet, ill or even dead in the morning often results in a culture of protecting themselves against criticism. This can lead to an indiscriminate and over-frequent practice of checking. In the study it was found that staff would often routinely check most or all residents whether they required this or not. This often disturbed the residents unnecessarily. It was noteworthy that during the course of the study some residents asked the researchers to ask staff not to check them. The unnecessary disturbance caused some people to become agitated and then experience difficulty going back to sleep.

> I am fast asleep and then they open the door and put on the light and I jump awake, my heart jumps and then I cannot get back to sleep.

The feelings of some residents in relation to checking was expressed well by one female resident who commented:

> Oh yes we have got this little old lady who walks up and down here, and what she doesn't bring to me is nobody's business… But sometimes she will just say 'checking'. Well, she did the last time. I kind of wakened up, she says 'checking'…some people don't hear her, and I think there's a man now sometimes wanders up and down. I don't know. (Kerr *et al.* 2008, p.32)

This resident was clearly bothered by this intrusion as she went back to it much later:

> I think I would (lock the door), just to let whoever is doing it know *that they* can't get in. And that of

course would waken me right up, you know I am just conscious that something has happened, if you hear the click, that's all, but I couldn't tell you who it is. And the nurses as far as I know don't do a round, I don't think they... It wakes...I don't know, I just say who is it, you see, and you get the voice 'just checking'...she is small, a little thing. And somebody said she is quite harmless, I said well maybe she is, I don't know. (Kerr *et al.* 2008, p.32)

Imagine the following scenario.

## CASE STUDY 12

You are on holiday, staying in a hotel. You are tucked up in bed fast asleep. The door to your bedroom opens and a stranger is standing there. They smile at you and say your name but you have no idea who they are. They come over to your bed and take the bed covers off and start to feel around your bottom.

It is not hard to appreciate the sense of invasion, abuse and panic that this will probably induce. It also easy to imagine your response. You would probably scream, shout, hit out, fight back, grab your clothes and try to run away.

A person with dementia may very well think that they are staying in a hotel when they are in fact in a care home, and because of their dementia they may well not recognise the staff member who comes to their room. It is worth noting that the responses you would have, if this happened to you, are often labelled as 'challenging behaviour' when residents have the same reaction.

Some residents, however, welcomed the staff coming to their rooms. Those who felt that the checking was kept to a minimum and not intrusive saw it as a reassurance.

I know they would come and see that you're OK, you know, during the night. I just turn over. I know who it is.

But she just opens the door and looks to see everything's all right and away she goes. It doesn't matter. Because if I wasn't feeling too great, then I could always tell her. (Kerr *et al.* 2008, p.32)

The way in which people are checked is also important. Kerr *et al.* found a number of checking procedures that gave cause for concern.

## CASE STUDY 13

Caroline was fast asleep in her room. She had been sleeping from about 11 p.m. At 2 a.m. a staff member opened her bedroom door, turned on the main light and called out in a loud voice, 'Caroline, wake up now, I have come to check you.' Caroline was heard to cry out. The nurse did not continue to speak and reassure her but simply went into the now brightly lit room and made her check of Caroline's incontinence pad.

The checking process must be carried out with sufficient sensitivity, and managers need to be aware of the manner in which this practice is being performed.

Many staff will provide calm, sensitive checking, but this needs to be provided consistently by all. Staff need to be provided with low-light torches or dimmer switches that they can use initially so as not to startle people and to give them time to adjust their vision. People also need to be talked to calmly and quietly in a soothing way that causes the least distress. This distress was often exacerbated by the lack of gender-appropriate interventions. That the night shift usually comprises a small staff group narrows the choice for residents in relation to gender. If there are only two staff and one is a man and the woman is busy, then the resident will be tended by a man even if this is very uncomfortable for the resident.

I did ring and he came and I said, 'I would rather have a lady please.' 'Oh what's wrong with me?' or

something. And I said I haven't anything against you,
I just would prefer a lady. It was because I needed to
use the toilet I think for something' (female resident).
(Kerr *et al.* 2008, p.31)

Core to the philosophy of care given in care homes is that residents
should have choice. It seems, however, that it may well be possible
to choose whether to eat meat or fish, to go to bed at 8 o'clock
or midnight, or to join in a group activity or not, but it is not
possible to make a choice about a much more meaningful and
intimate practice. For many women, and perhaps particularly older
women, to be touched intimately by a man or even seen naked
by a man other than their husband, a doctor or a nurse would be
embarrassing and even shameful.

Where there is unnecessary, routine, indiscriminate, non-
person-centred checking, this needs to be eliminated from night-
time practices. Not only does this distress residents, but it also
takes staff away from other activities in which they might be better
employed.

## Managing continence at night

The management of incontinence is a key component in the
reduction of and consequent improvement in checking routines
and practices. It is also fundamental to providing good-quality care
and quality of life for care home residents.

Incontinence is not a part of normal ageing (Dugan *et al.* 2001;
Landi *et al.* 2003) but is often accepted in care home settings
as an inevitable aspect of the ageing process in general or the
onset of dementia in particular. The Royal College of Physicians
(2006) reported that 40–70 per cent of care home residents
were incontinent, and this number is increasing. This rise may
be attributable to factors such as the increased age of care home
residents and the increased number of people with dementia in
care homes, but it might also be simply the result of a lack of

suitable staff training and the use of inappropriate systems and resources.

Being incontinent is more than just a physical concern; there are also social and emotional implications for people whose continence is not well managed. Individuals who experience incontinence often feel embarrassed and frustrated (Ouslander *et al.* 1993) and this may affect their behaviour and mood.

### CASE STUDY 14

Meg is a frail older woman who has lived in the care home for six months. When she moved in she was continent with support, through regular assistance to go to the bathroom. During the night she tended to need to get up to go to the bathroom in the early hours and needed to call for help to do this. More recently the night staff have been using continence pads for Meg, arguing that it's better for Meg to get a full night's sleep. However, in practice, Meg is woken every two hours by staff checking her pad to make sure she is dry.

A continence nurse visiting the home asked about night-time continence and discussed Meg's case, suggesting that while Meg still had continence she should be supported to go to the toilet at regular intervals during the day and when she called for help. If this ability was lost, then at night the use of higher-capacity pads would mean that staff would not have to check Meg was dry during the night. A record of toileting was established to include both day and night-time so that her changing needs were easily seen by all staff.

## Continence care as an important issue

One of the most difficult aspects of care in care homes settings is managing continence. In general, staff often report dealing with urinary incontinence to be one of the most stressful and difficult conditions for which they care, and they perceive that they spend a disproportionate amount of time on this area of care work (Ouslander and Schnelle 1995; Sorbye *et al.* 2008). Increasing levels of incontinence amongst care home residents has a major impact on both residents' health and the cost of care (Ouslander *et al.* 1995). There is a clear association between moderate or severe cognitive impairment, usually associated with dementia, and incontinence and dependency in toileting and other activities of daily living.

Care homes are likely to have a high prevalence of severe and uncontrolled symptoms of urinary incontinence and this requires support and input from specialist continence services. A random sample of local authority and private care homes (Peet *et al.* 1996) found that 87 per cent of the homes used pads, but 83 per cent had daytime toileting programmes to promote continence care. However, only 52 per cent of these homes practised night-time toileting programmes. Only 49 per cent used clear toilet signs or had toilets made easily visible. This shows a greater emphasis being placed on the use of continence pads than on the implementation of toileting programmes to promote continence. Good toileting programmes were found in only 32 per cent of homes surveyed. Very few of the homes had accessed any support such as continence nurses (only 30% of homes) or specialist continence doctors (9% of homes).

Poor continence care has a number of negative consequences for residents. It can lead to a loss of skin quality and prevent pressure sores healing (Ouslander, Greengold and Chen 1987). At night if people are not adequately supervised or aided when they get up to go to the toilet, there is an increased risk of them falling if they find it difficult to walk, have poor balance or are visually impaired (Ouslander *et al.* 1993). Good lighting is very important in this regard, so that the person can not only see the way to the toilet but also see the toilet door and the toilet itself when they get there.

Many care home residents have 'dependent continence' and are continent only through the efforts of the carer (Palmer *et al.*

1997). People who require help moving to the toilet or when using the toilet are at greater risk of incontinence. A spell in hospital is also a high risk factor for becoming more dependent on continence support. Frail older adults and those with dementia may need assistance going to the toilet as they stop being able to recognise that they need the toilet or because mobility difficulties prevent them from getting to the toilet without help (Sorbye *et al.* 2008, p.41). In many cases the most important factor in helping to reduce incontinence is nurses having the time and the training to detect potentially remediable causes of incontinence – effective management is really focused on assisted toileting on a regular prompt basis.

During the night, making sure residents are dry and clean is essential. Often the level of checking in the night is linked to a concern to keep a resident dry, but frequent checking for dryness can also interfere with good sleep. One of the difficulties during the night is that noise from the staff and other residents and light and noise from staff-initiated incontinence care and checking routines can increase the risk of waking the resident (Schnelle, Cruise and Alessi 1998). With the correct assessment, support and provisions, good continence care does not require high levels of checking and the associated disturbance that causes.

It is important that individuals have been assessed for their continence needs at night as well as during the day, and that the toileting routine or continence care through the use of larger-volume pads are used to minimise sleep disruption while considering moisture exposure that could affect skin health.

As continence products develop and improve through the use of superabsorbent materials, there is more evidence that appropriate night pads are effective for longer periods. A comprehensive study in 2003 examined the impact on dryness and skin if pads were changed through the night (every four hours) and when they were not changed through the night at all (Fader, Clarke-O'Neill and Cook 2003). This study found no evidence that less frequent changing had any effect on skin erythema (abnormal redness of skin) or pH, although the less-frequently changed residents did have wetter skin which could make it more vulnerable to friction and abrasion, especially if faecal incontinence was left.

One of the most important messages from this study, related to an unintended finding, was that in none of the homes in which they completed the study was there a systematic method for assessing, recording or communicating the night-time continence needs of residents. The authors highly recommended as a basic and central requirement that documentation was used and shared by staff to record residents' individual needs for types of pads and frequency of checking and changing (Fader *et al.* 2003). This needs to be part of a night-time care plan that is provided for each resident as part of a care strategy. Night staff must be the people who decide what type and number of pads a resident requires. Kerr *et al.* (2008) found that in some homes it was the day staff who made decisions about the provision of pads. Their decisions were based on their experience of the residents' needs during the day, meaning that often inadequate provision was made for the night-time needs of the person. Night-time continence needs are often different to those in the day, and these differences are often overlooked even when continence advice and training are provided (Kerr *et al.* 2008). Night staff commented that such training as they had received had described and concentrated on daytime issues of continence management.

Kerr *et al.* (2008) highlighted a number of strategies that increased person-centred night work and in particular more person-centred checking habits:

- Managers spent some time with night staff between midnight and 4 o'clock. This enabled managers to develop a better understanding of the checking routines that were in place. It also enabled night staff to talk to the manager and discuss reasons for the various practices.

- The implementation of a night-time key worker system meant that each member of the night staff had responsibility for certain residents. It was their job to know more about that resident, their needs and desires, as well as their night-time behaviour and habits. This also, of course, included the need to carry out an assessment of the person's continence levels and need for checking.

- The indiscriminate checking of residents dropped with better assessment of continence needs at night.

- The introduction of night-time care plans. All homes will have care plans for the 24 hours of care. These are, often, not sufficiently night-time specific. The development of plans that are about night care issues means that staff can target specific issues that affect residents at night and will therefore be more sensitive to the night care needs, particularly around checking.

Drawing on the work of Kerr *et al.* (2008), Highland Council Social Work Services have developed a template for an overnight care plan (Figure 6.1). This is a good example of a simple but effective format that should be regularly reviewed.

The effective use of a plan such as that in Figure 6.1 assumes a level of consistency and ability amongst night staff. It is, however, unfortunate that agency and bank staff rarely know the residents well, and such a lack of relationship and knowledge is likely to be more problematic during the night when staffing levels are lower than during the day, with less opportunity for permanent staff to fill the gaps. As indicated in Chapter 2, night staff receive less training than day staff and so are less well informed of certain issues, including incontinence and dementia. Improved training in these areas will increase staff confidence in their ability to make assessments of the need for checking.

OVERNIGHT CARE PLAN

Name:

Room number:

Night key worker:

Night-time routine:

Getting ready for bed

(Include in general what time, how much assistance required, etc.)

Is medication required overnight?

Is the resident self-medicating?

What help is required?

Is a night check required?

Is the resident able to call for assistance using the help call system?

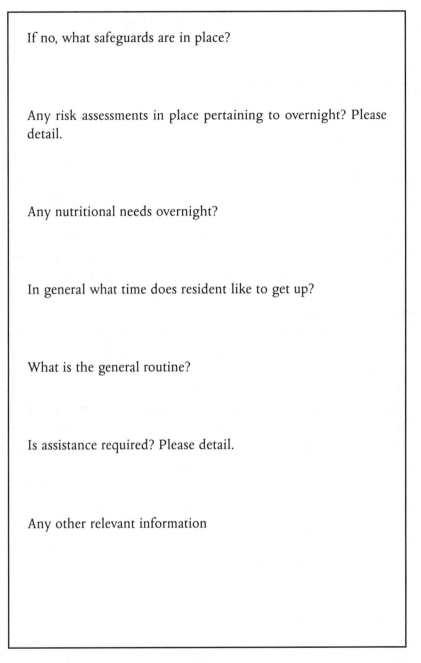

If no, what safeguards are in place?


Any risk assessments in place pertaining to overnight? Please detail.


Any nutritional needs overnight?


In general what time does resident like to get up?


What is the general routine?


Is assistance required? Please detail.


Any other relevant information

Figure 6.1 Example of a care plan for the use by night staff

# The use of technology

The use of assistive technology will be discussed in more detail in Chapter 8. It is pertinent here, however, to consider the role that it can play in both reducing the frequency of checking and making checking more person-centred and specifically targeted. The use of pressure mats and infrared detectors in people's bedrooms could alert staff to the fact that a person was out of bed. This may or may not require a response, but it would mean that staff do not always have to physically check what is happening. There is also technology that allows people's routines, such the use of the toilet at night, to be recorded and monitored. The person's movements would only become alarming and require staff intervention if and when the person varies their routine – if, for example, they do not return to bed within the expected time frame. A wireless sensor network such as ALARM-NET would facilitate this monitoring (Wood *et al.* 2006).

Miura *et al.* (2008) used radio frequency identification devices (RFID) such as tagged slippers to monitor people's movements. The use of slippers or other similar tags allowed staff to develop a picture of a person's movement and also to detect when things changed. McCullagh *et al.* (2009, p.2) suggest that 'Understanding the pattern of movement at night-time may improve the safety of elderly people who are at risk of falling'. Certainly such knowledge may enable staff to feel more confident about not checking so often. Holmes *et al.* (2007), however, found that such information actually very slightly increased checking. This may simply be an indication that staff need to be supported not to react to people's movements unless there is real cause for concern. Clearly this is an area that requires more research.

# Summary

Night staff play an important role in ensuring that residents are safe, that sleep is promoted as appropriate and that people's medical, social and emotional needs are attended to. Checking people through the night is part of this role, but it is essential that such checking is only done when necessary, planned on the basis of individual needs and done quietly and with sensitivity.

Some residents are comforted by staff visiting them at night and are not disturbed by the checking process; others find it frightening and disorientating to have someone come into their room when they are asleep.

Offering residents a choice of the gender of the staff taking care of them at night is important, although this can be difficult as the night shift can be a small staff team.

The management of continence is a key component in the reduction of and consequent improvement in checking routines and practices. Wherever possible, people should be supported to use the toilet at night rather than use continence pads. Adequate supervision of and help for people who get up to go to the toilet is essential and will also reduce the risk of falls. Good lighting is important so that people can see the way to the toilet, and see the toilet door and the toilet itself when they get there.

# Chapter 7

# Eating and Drinking Through the Night

Eating and drinking are not perhaps the first things that come to mind when thinking of night-time care, but in this section we focus on how to make sure that people in care homes have appropriate food and drink throughout the night. Many care home providers would endorse the following statement: 'The resident has a right to have their nutritional needs and wishes met irrespective of the time of day. It is the responsibility of each member of staff to ensure these needs and wishes are met' (Bupa 2007).

This chapter will describe the various issues that need to be addressed to ensure that such an aspiration becomes fact.

The following will be addressed:

- the changing nutritional needs of older people
- recognising the risk factors for older people not eating and drinking enough
- some practical things that can help older people to eat and drink well at night

- some examples of types of food and drink that are suitable at night
- the impact dementia can have on how people eat and drink.

## The changing nutritional needs of older people

As people grow older, their patterns of eating and drinking and their ability and desire to eat and drink can change. For people living in care homes there are a number of additional factors that affect their eating and drinking. These can include health concerns and being ill; emotional concerns such as feeling isolated and being depressed, worried or getting used to living in a care home; issues relating to care, such as not having enough staff to help people eat, providing poor quality or unappetising food. Many of these have only been researched in relation to daytime care. However, they still have implications for care through the night.

### CASE STUDY 15

Edith came into the care home after a stay in hospital, and her family noted after visits that she seemed to be very thin and to have lost her appetite. At first staff said that it was due to Edith getting frailer, but her daughter persisted and the staff completed a three-week round of weighing Edith and monitoring her eating and drinking. They found that she was malnourished and that Edith was finding it very difficult to eat on her own using cutlery. The care home put in place a supported eating plan based on finger foods supplemented with high calorie drinks. These drinks were also available throughout the night when Edith was often awake in the early hours. These early-hour drinks and snack times also offered the staff a time to get to know Edith and to help her settle into the care home more, talking through some of the changes with her.

# Eating and drinking

Hydration and drinking enough fluid are basic concerns in the care of older people. It has been found that older people in hospital and in care homes are at a high risk of dehydration (Armstrong-Esther *et al.* 1996; Haan *et al.* 1997; Morely and Kraenzle 1994; Weinberg *et al.* 1994). The 'MUST' ('Malnutrition Universal Screening Tool') Report* (Elia 2003) highlighted that up to 40 per cent of those admitted to hospital are underweight – evidence shows that many will lose further weight whilst in hospital – and up to 60 per cent of hospital patients are clinically malnourished. Furthermore, up to 50 per cent of patients in care or residential homes, up to 30 per cent of patients attending outpatient clinics and GP surgeries, and up to 14 per cent of elderly people not in hospital or care are either malnourished or at risk of malnourishment. The 'MUST' was the first universal nutritional screening tool for adults, a landmark development in addressing the damaging effects of malnutrition.

Many older people no longer feel thirsty even when dehydrated (Miller 1997; Morley 2000; Phillips, Johnston and Gray 1993) and their senses of taste and smell can become impaired. Conditions such as stroke can additionally decrease the thirst response (Morley and Silver 1995). The risks associated with dehydration are often linked to the onset of febrile illnesses where there is a fever or diarrhoea when dehydration can develop very quickly.

Dehydration can be an indication of poor quality of care. Having enough to eat and drink is clearly linked to supporting good health. The following list is an indication of some of the more common consequences of malnutrition and dehydration:

---

\*      The 'MUST' Report (2003) by the Malnutrition Advisory Group, a standing committee of BAPEN (the British Association for Parenteral and Enteral Nutrition) which also launched the 'MUST' ('Malnutrition Universal Screening Tool').

- apathy
- memory loss
- poor wound healing
- breathing difficulties
- skin problems and sores, pressure ulcers
- cardiac difficulties
- increased risk of infection
- prolonged complications after operations
- confusion
- musculoskeletal difficulties including weakness and poor coordination
- high risk of falls
- reduced salivary flow
- periodontal sepsis
- constipation
- increased illness, disease and mortality.

(Morley 1999; Morley and Silver 1995; Ship and Fischer 1997; Wilson 1998)

Not enough to eat and drink through the day can result in residents being up in the night hungry or thirsty; unnecessary fluid intake during the day can increase nocturia (Asplund and Aberg 1991), so clearly finding a balance to meet the needs of the individual is a central part of care. There is often concern amongst staff about the amount of fluid people should have. Staff worry that too much fluid intake will lead to night-time incontinence. The temptation, therefore, is to restrict the intake, especially during the evening. The Modified Food Guide Pyramid recommends that people aged 70 and over have a minimum of eight glasses of water per day (Russell, Rasmussen and Lichtenstein 1999). However, more recently, Morley's (2000) review of evidence in relation to hydration recommended six rather than eight glasses of water for healthy older people, but for this intake to increase to eight glasses for older people experiencing illnesses caused by fever. It is important that staff monitor and, if necessary, supervise fluid intake. Simply giving people a drink does not guarantee that they drink it.

Important things to think about in practice, both during the day and at night, are:

- Help a person have regular drinks.
- Don't just leave a person with a drink, but check that they can drink it and have drunk some or all of it.
- When giving drinks through the night, be aware of the balance between fluid intake and the need to go to the toilet.

As in hydration, nutritional concerns for people in care homes during the night are closely related to daytime intake, activities and health factors. The most common nutritional problems for care home residents are weight loss, malnutrition and associated lack of protein which reduces energy levels. Unless weight loss is due to the end-stage of a disease, most weight loss in older people can be treated. However, it has to be first recognised, and nutritional problems are often not identified or recognised sufficiently in care home settings. Obesity is much less common in care homes but, given the demographics of obesity in younger generations, it is something to note for the future as it can be associated with immobility, decreased functional status and the development of pressure sores (Morley and Silver 1995).

Many people in care homes are dependent eaters, in that they need practical assistance with eating. Some people cannot get the food from plate to mouth. This may be because they have tremors or because meat is too tough to cut or to chew. It can also be due to the effect of dementia resulting in difficulty locating the mouth or maintaining the purposeful movement necessary to get the food from plate to mouth. Different cutlery may help, but often people require staff assistance.

The social conditions of mealtimes may also affect appetite. The room can be very noisy and busy. Dining space is often shared with other people who may have nasogastric tubes or poor eating habits which cause distress to other people eating in the room.

People who are pacing and walking about during the day will need a higher calorie intake to make up for the energy used.

## Recognising risk factors

The most important practical thing is to be able to recognise risk factors for individuals and be able to take action. It is essential that there is 24-hour monitoring, and night staff need to be equipped and alert to people's night-time nutritional needs. The list below highlights some of the most common factors to look out for:

- Lower resting metabolic rate.
- Reduced food intake.
- Decreased desire to eat through loss of smell and taste or through the social conditions of eating. Appetites may also be smaller and people may only be able to eat a small amount before feeling full.
- Lack of choice and variation in food, or culturally inappropriate food.
- Illnesses such as chronic infections or chronic heart disease.
- Adverse drug effects that can cause nausea, constipation, etc.
- Constipation linked to the general slowing down of the gastrointestinal system. This can cause severe pain.
- Depression which is known to occur in 8–38 per cent of residents (Fitten *et al.* 1989) and closely relates to 'failure to thrive' (Katz *et al.* 1993).
- Poor oral health – studies show at least 80 per cent of care home residents have significant teeth loss (Thomson,

Brown and Williams 1992) which, makes chewing difficult.

- Need for help to eat.
- Chewing and swallowing problems.

Information is crucial and everyone, both night and day staff, has a role to play. Those assisting people to eat will know about the amount and type of food each person has taken. The chart in Figure 7.1 can be a very simple way of gathering basic information on intake. Most of the data in this chart will be gathered by day staff but it is very important that night staff also maintain the chart and that information is shared between staff groups.

Screening and monitoring is particularly important during the first two to three months after a resident moves into a home. It is recommended (Morley and Silver 1995) that individuals are weighed biweekly during their first month. This is especially important for those returning from a stay in hospital as many of these individuals are at high risk and will usually need nutritional interventions such as food supplements to regain weight. It is possible that such monitoring can be part of the evening and bedtime routine and undertaken by night as well as day staff, providing that there are effective recording and communication systems in place to make sure that the information is shared and, where necessary, acted upon.

Once the needs of a person have been assessed, then there are a number of practical things that can be done to support better eating and drinking, including using times during the night when people may be awake to have snacks and drinks. Some of these ideas are outlined in the next section.

## Practical things that can help

There is a range of things that can be used to support better eating and drinking. Those we have outlined here can be used during the

| Day/Date/ Time | What food was offered? | What food was eaten? | What drink was offered? | What drink was drunk? |
|---|---|---|---|---|
|  |  |  |  |  |
|  |  |  |  |  |
|  |  |  |  |  |
|  |  |  |  |  |
|  |  |  |  |  |
|  |  |  |  |  |

Figure 7.1 Chart for monitoring food and drink intake

evening and night as well as during the day. Some measures are quite practical, such as:

- having enough staff to help people eat
- use of specially adapted cutlery
- upright postures, especially for people with swallowing problems.

Other measures can include the advice of speech and language therapists (SALTs) and using special diets that are aimed at avoiding under-nutrition as a priority. Where a resident is losing weight, liquid meal replacements or nutritional supplements will help and should be tried in most cases before anything more invasive is considered.

The role of physical activity is important to consider as part of care and quality of life. Activity has numerous positive effects such as keeping muscles working, improving strength and nutrition-related effects including improved appetite and protein intake, improved bowel function and reduced constipation, and the possibility of an improved immune system (Shephard 1995). Appropriate levels of activity during the day can help improve appetite and also aid tiredness and sleep.

## Food and drinks for night-time

In many homes, however, there are logistical problems with meeting residents' need to have food at night. Very often the kitchen is locked and there is no or little access to any alternative food or cooking facilities.

It is important that night staff see part of their role as supporting people to eat if this is wanted and needed. All too often this is not the case and night-time eating is kept to a minimum.

In fact, night-time may well provide an ideal opportunity to help people obtain their daily nutritional needs and requirements. For many people, and for people with dementia in particular, the night-time provides the quiet, calm, one-to-one support needed to help people with eating problems. Compare the hustle and bustle of a care home at 4 o'clock in the afternoon and 4 o'clock in the morning. It is evident which time is calmer and probably more conducive to slow, unhurried eating and drinking.

The type of food offered at night needs to be well planned. Someone has to be responsible for the stocking and safekeeping of night-time food. There are obviously some issues around health and safety, the access and storage of food and the amount of time night staff have to prepare it. As there is not a cook on at night, food offered has to be easily prepared. However, there really is no reason why the food on offer at night should not be wide-ranging, interesting and culturally and individually sensitive.

The list below gives some examples of some simple foods that can be offered through the night, including food that can be presented as 'finger food'. These are just examples, staff will be able to think of many other examples, and indeed many that will be sensitive to the diets of their particular residents.

## Bread and cereals

- buttered toast fingers
- buttered muffins/crumpet
- buttered buns
- rolls and butter
- fruit loaf
- tea bread
- sandwiches
- crackers and butter
- gingerbread

## Meat, fish, cheese and other protein alternatives

- sliced meat, cut up into pieces
- cheese on toast

- fried bean curd cubes
- fish fingers
- quartered boiled egg
- cheese cubes
- vegetable or soya sausage

## Vegetables

- carrot sticks or coins, cooked
- quartered tomato
- sliced cucumber
- celery sticks

## Fruit

- banana
- strawberries
- melon slices
- grapes
- sliced apple or pear
- mandarin orange segments

## Snacks

- dried apricots/prunes (stones removed)
- peanut butter sandwiches
- pâté on toast
- jelly cubes
- Marmite on toast
- ice cream in cones

(Adapted from Ford 1996)

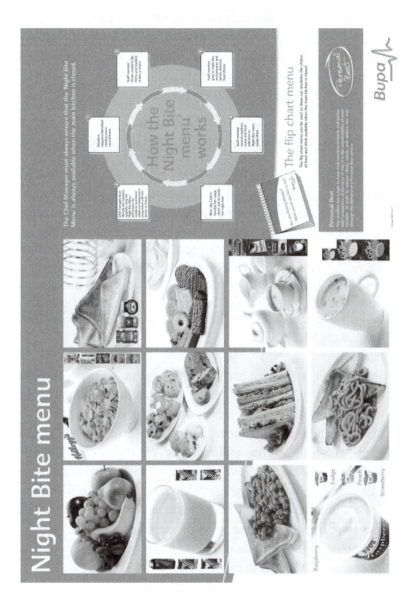

Figure 7.2 'Night Bite menu' (Bupa 2009)

A simple way to remind staff of the need for appropriate nutrition at night is to have a poster on display in the kitchen. Figure 7.2 is a good example of this. The use of photo menu cards showing different food and drink enables residents to make a choice even when they have problems with speech.

## The impact of dementia on eating and drinking

### CASE STUDY 16

Bob was sitting with other residents in the lounge as a member of staff brought a trolley around with an evening drink and toast. Bob was given a cup of tea and a slice of white toast and it was placed to the side of him on a small table. About 20 minutes later the trolley went around again and Bob's untouched tea and toast was gathered back up. A few minutes later Bob started to ask for a drink of tea. The member of staff said, 'No, Bob, you never drink it, we've just been around.'

In this section we discuss the impact of having dementia on eating and drinking; many of the health and practical examples in this section, however, are also relevant to all care home residents.

Having dementia makes eating and drinking increasingly difficult. As with any care home resident, it is important not to assume that any weight loss in someone with dementia is due to the illness. Although in the latter stages of the condition people will inevitably lose weight, in the early and mid stages this weight loss is more likely to be due to inadequate support with eating and drinking. Research has found that up to 50 per cent of people with dementia can be malnourished (Watson 1994).

## Practical/physical changes linked to dementia may mean that a person is:

- unable to use cutlery
- having problems with tremors and so will be unable to get food to their mouth
- unable to unwrap or peel food and may try to eat it wrapped
- unable to sit for meals
- extremely slow in eating.

## Physiological changes mean the person may:

- have difficulty chewing
- have difficulty swallowing
- lose their sense of smell and taste
- lose their appetite
- have problems/pain with their teeth, gums and dentures
- show a preference for sweet food
- store food in their mouth as they don't know how to swallow.

## Emotional and cognitive factors mean the person may:

- be easily distracted
- forget to eat or forget that they have eaten
- eat with their hands
- be unable to communicate hunger or thirst
- be unable to see and remember food or drink that is not directly in front of them
- eat things that are not food
- have difficulty making choices.

(Adapted from Hall 1994)

If someone has any of the above difficulties, it is essential that professional advice is sought. Speech and language therapists (SALTs) are able to give advice about what to use and how, where and when to support people to eat and drink. Ideally, this need will have been addressed by the day staff, but it is important that information about people's night-time eating and drinking is communicated to the SALT and also that any information from the SALT is communicated back to night staff.

When deciding on when to seek a referral, the chart in Figure 7.3 can be used. This chart should be shared by day and night staff. Ideally, the referral should be made when the diagnosis of dementia is given and should not wait until difficulties arise.

The SALT will give advice about the texture of food as well as the types of food that need to be given. It is very important that night staff have such foods available. The list of finger foods on pages 87–88 should be helpful, but staff also need to know about how to change food consistency safely. Breakfast cereals soaked in warm milk to soften the texture, fruit and vegetables that are well cooked with no stones or skins, and dairy products such as yoghurt and cheese dishes with sauces and smoothies can be appropriate foods. Most of these are foods that can be available through the night even if the kitchen is not available.

People with dementia may not be ready to sit and eat three meals a day. They often need to eat small amounts and more frequently – a sort of grazing approach to eating. This may mean that by the evening people have not eaten all that they need for their daily intake and this needs to be supplemented through the night, if possible. Someone who becomes increasingly sedentary or restless will have different energy requirements at different times of the day. A big breakfast followed by a main meal at lunchtime and a light snack at supper/tea may be appropriate for the sedentary person, but the person who paces may need to eat fairly constantly. The pattern of three set meals a day will often have to be abandoned in favour of a more person-centred approach to providing food and opportunities to eat. It is important to work

## Please indicate if, and how often, the person exhibits the following:

| | Never | Sometimes | Always |
|---|---|---|---|
| Coughing or choking during or after meal/drink times | | | |
| Dehydration | | | |
| Chest infections | | | |
| Urinary tract infections | | | |
| Change in voice quality – 'gurgly' or wet voice when speaking | | | |
| Drooling of saliva/food/fluid | | | |
| Nasal regurgitation | | | |
| Gasping for breath at meals | | | |
| Pockets of food around inside of mouth | | | |
| Fatigue at mealtimes – taking a long time to eat and drink | | | |
| More sleepy than usual after meal | | | |
| Suspected discomfort when swallowing | | | |
| Change of colour in the face | | | |
| Sounds of respiratory difficulty | | | |
| Rapid heart rate | | | |
| High temperature | | | |

Completed by:          Date:          Next completion date:

If you have responded in either the 'sometimes' or the 'always' column for any factor, please contact your speech and language therapist to arrange a full assessment.

(Taken from 'Eating and Drinking Safely – a concern for us all'. A Joint Surrey and Borders Partnership NHS Trust SALT and Dietetic project.)

Figure 7.3 Chart to monitor eating and drinking difficulties

out when people are most lucid and most able to eat and drink and to make sure that it is at this time that they are offered their most nutritious meal. If the night staff find that someone is waking at night because he is hungry and wanting to eat, they need to communicate with day staff to check that sufficient attention is being given to the person's food and liquid intake. Often because there is no consistent monitoring or recording of people's eating and drinking throughout the day, the night-time waking because of hunger is not appropriately addressed.

Often day staff do not feel able to give the time and attention that people with dementia require to enable them to eat their meal. It can take someone with dementia 40 minutes to eat a standard meal. This is a long time for staff to support. For this reason food is cleared away often before the person has actually finished. It is worth noting here that because of the time it takes people with dementia to eat their meal, the use of 'cook and chill', where food is cooked centrally and then distributed and reheated by the staff, is not recommended. This food cannot be reheated once it has gone cold and residents are often presented with a cold, congealed meal that is offensive and often inedible. The poor nutritional intake can then have an impact on people's night-time behaviour.

During the day, meal times are important social events, with emotional and social significance, as well as an opportunity to eat and drink. Sometimes this opportunity is lost on the person with dementia who can find meal times stressful. Helping someone eat or drink during the night, when there is less activity and staff can provide important emotional and social support, should not be dismissed without some consideration of the benefits to the person.

## Summary

Eating and drinking are not perhaps the first things to come to mind when thinking of night-time care, but all residents have the right to have their nutritional needs and wishes met irrespective of the time of day. People living in care homes can experience a number of factors that affect their eating and drinking, including health worries, emotional concerns such as feeling isolated and being depressed, adjusting to living in a care home, not having enough staff to help people eat, and the provision of poor-quality or unappetising food. This can mean that people might be hungry during the night. Night staff have to be equipped with the resources to meet this need. They need access to the type of food that is suitable at night, and in particular to food that is suitable for people with dementia.

Changes linked to dementia may mean that people experience many practical, physiological and emotional difficulties in eating and drinking – they may not be able to sit and eat three meals a day, so it is important that they eat small amounts and more often – a grazing approach to eating. The quiet evening and night can be ideal times to spend with people with dementia helping them to eat.

Chapter 8

# The Care Home Environment at Night

The night-time environment supports two different groups of people who are trying to achieve two different regimes, routines and experiences. For the staff, the environment is a place of work. It is an environment in which they have to be alert, organised, responsible and mobile. For the patients/residents, the night-time environment is essentially one that is intended to support sleep, rest, little or no activity and a great deal of dependence. These two potentially conflicting needs can sometimes come into sharp contrast and render the environment unsuitable for some or all of the people in it. This chapter, however, will focus on the environmental needs of the residents/patients.

There is a substantial body of knowledge and literature about environmental design and the social and emotional aspects of the environment best suited to older people and people with dementia living in care homes (Brawley 1997; Calkins 1988; Cantley and Wilson 2003; Cohen and Day 1993; Cohen and Weisman 1991; Judd, Marshall and Phippen 1998; Utton 2006). Much of this focuses on daytime environments. Daytime environmental factors will often be relevant to night-time environments, but there are some aspects of the night-time environment that need to be specifically addressed.

The role of the environment is:

- to enable staff to support people with the least amount of disturbance
- to facilitate residents' sleep
- to reduce or prevent people's agitation
- to help people find their way around the building at night
- to help people have a restful night, whether awake or not
- to keep people safe and comfortable.

Unfortunately, the night-time physical environment often fails to meet all of the above criteria.

## CASE STUDY 17

Maurice, a man in his 70s with a diagnosis of dementia, would wake at night and shout and scream. He would bang on his bedroom door, calling out to tell people to take cover. Sometimes he would be found in the corridor saying he needed to get into the garden. He was very distressed and staff attempts to get him back to bed were met with increased agitation and sometimes with aggression as he tried to push them out of his way. He would shout out 'Mum' and 'David'.

Maurice had lived in London with his mother and brother David throughout the Second World War. He had experienced the German bombing of the city and had been at home at the time of the Blitz.

The buzzers that went off during the night in the home would penetrate his sleep and wake him, just as the air raid sirens had done when he was a boy. Because of his dementia, his reality was that he was now living back in the 1940s in London during the Blitz. His desperate need to get into the garden was to get into the Anderson Bunker, which people built in their gardens as protection from the bombs.

This case study illustrates well the way in which aspects of the night-time environment can not only fail to support positive experiences and a sense of well-being but also cause distress, fear and behaviours that are often described as 'challenging'.

This chapter will address environmental issues that, whilst relevant during the day, have particular importance at night. Issues addressed will be:

- noise
- light
- flooring
- signage and colour
- mirrors
- assistive technology.

## Noise

People often find intrusive noise distressing. The recognition of this has led to expectations around noise management and reduction being included in care standards, for example:

> Standard 4:3: 'You can expect that the premises are kept free from intrusive sounds throughout.' (Scottish Executive 2005, p.19)

This is obviously an issue relevant to the whole 24 hours of care. It becomes particularly important when considering the night-time environment, when almost any noise has the potential to be experienced as intrusive.

In any setting where a number of people are living together, noise is going to be an issue. In care homes where as many as 40-plus people are living and working within one environment, the amount of noise generated is going to be beyond that normally experienced within someone's own home. For older people who may well have hearing problems and/or dementia, the noise level becomes more concerning than for the younger non-hearing-impaired staff.

The use of hearing aids often means that all the noises are equally amplified, and this can be very distressing for people. People with dementia are particularly prone to becoming agitated and distressed by noise levels. They have a decreased ability to filter out unwanted noise (Jacques and Jackson 2000) and so cannot differentiate between sounds, and consequently they find it hard to prioritise and concentrate on specific noises. The sound of the TV, the dishwasher, the staff and residents talking and the buzzers going can be quite overwhelming. At night, noise is still an issue but one that is compounded by the need for residents to sleep.

The intermittent exposure to noise is known to contribute to sleep disturbance (Fiorentino and Ancoli-Israel 2006). Schnelle *et al.* (1993a and 1993b) also found that 50 per cent of awakenings of more than four minutes in duration were associated with either noise or light. It is therefore essential to consider noise and light levels if the sleep of residents/patients is going to be supported rather than disrupted. Light levels are considered later in this chapter.

Sometimes it is hard to appreciate how much noise there is at night. Staff, unlike residents, are busy, active and not hearing-impaired, nor do they have dementia. It has proved quite instructive for night staff to undertake the following exercise.

Sit in a 'quiet' space for 10 minutes. Close your eyes and take notice of all the different noises you hear. Listen for even the quieter distant sounds. Think about what is making the noise and if there are a number of ways of interpreting the sound. For example, what might be causing a creak? If people are talking, can you hear what they are saying?

People who do this exercise are usually surprised at the amount and variety of noise that exists. The next problem is to work out how to reduce it.

Kerr *et al.* (2008) found that there are unacceptable levels of noise at night. The need to promote sleep, particularly for people who, because of their age and conditions, are often light sleepers, means that noise levels at night must be given priority. There are a number of causes of noise that need to be addressed if people are going to be given the best opportunity to sleep in peace. These include:

- buzzers
- staff activities
- plumbing and floorboards
- distressed residents.

## Buzzers

For most of us, if we want to make sure we wake up, we set an alarm clock which wakes us very efficiently. However, our alarms will not be as loud or as persistent as many buzzers in care homes. In some homes the buzzer gets louder and louder the longer it is on, and in some homes the buzzers cannot be turned off until a staff member reaches the resident's room. It's not surprising, then, that people wake up.

An alarm clock is used to tell us it is morning and that we need to get up. We should not be surprised, therefore, that people with dementia think the noise of the buzzer is telling them that they need to get up to go to work or get the children up, or, as in Maurice's case, attach distressing meaning to the noise.

There is no need for buzzers. The technology exists for staff to have pagers (or bleeps) that alert them to a person calling for attention. Where pagers are provided, it is essential that staff are supplied with new batteries. The use of flashing lights on a central board is an alternative that can be used to reduce the noise level, although there is the possibility that no one will be at the central point when the light flashes.

## Staff activities

Fiorentino and Ancoli-Israel (2006) found that noise levels were a major problem in nursing homes. They found that noise levels increased until midnight, then decreased from 1 a.m. to 4 a.m. 'The source of the noise was most often related to nursing staff speaking loudly or staff creating other noise with squeaking medication carts or pill crushing' (p.294).

Kerr *et al.* (2008) found that although some staff were sensitive to the need for quiet at night, other staff were not so aware. Sometimes even if staff recognised the need, they did not appreciate how loud their voices were in the still of the night. Some staff call to each other along a corridor or talk outside a bedroom. Obviously the need for staff to carry out essential nursing and caring activities creates noise. It is important that staff are aware of the need to try to control the level of noise made by these activities.

Jangling keys can be surprisingly noisy at night. They may also remind some residents of other situations when people had keys and control over them – for example, people who were in prison camps in the war or people with learning disabilities who have been in long-stay hospitals. The noise of opening and shutting doors, the noise of the laundry trolley being taken along corridors, the sound of plumbing when toilets were flushed and the creaking of floorboards as staff do their rounds can also be disturbing to residents.

The following comment from a staff member illustrates the possible consequence of such activities.

> And it is so true about the noise, because one night there was a nurse – a lovely nurse – she came down with a big trolley, and it sounded like thunder, and about five residents who don't usually get up actually got up and went up the stairs. (Kerr *et al.* 2008, p.45)

It is not always necessary to take the medicine, tea or laundry trolley along the corridor. Leaving it at the end and walking down to each room can significantly reduce the noise level.

### Plumbing, floorboards and creaking doors

As indicated above, the building itself can cause noise. Pipes running along the building from the laundry can be noisy in the night if the washing machines are on. Creaking floorboards are a potential source of distressing noise to people. Creaking doors and doors being shut with a bang can also be disturbing. Newer buildings can present the most problems with creaks and lack of soundproofing (Kerr *et al.* 2008). The following comment from a woman who had dementia is worth noting:

> That's one thing at the new building, the building gets so, what do they call it? You hear the noise more than you do in the old building. (p.33)

### Distressed residents

Fiorentino and Ancoli-Israel (2006) found that residents caused a minority of night-time noise. Undoubtedly noise *was* caused by residents, particularly if they were distressed. Much of this noise was the result of residents' distress, anxiety and fears being mishandled by staff who had little or no understanding of the perspective of people with dementia (Kerr *et al.* 2008). Consequently the staff responses often induced or escalated challenging behaviour. It was found that after good dementia training night staff had a better understanding of residents' night-time behaviour and so responded more appropriately, thus reducing distress and noise.

## Light levels

Of the 8,760 hours in a year, in the UK approximately 4,100 are in the dark. It is during the dark hours that night staff have an opportunity to control light levels. Utilising both natural daylight and electrical light, staff need to be aware of lighting levels and make sure that they enhance rather than damage the night-time experience of residents. Night-time light levels, like noise levels, will have a serious impact on people's ability to rest and sleep peacefully. The intermittent exposure to light throughout the night is known to contribute to sleep disturbance (Fiorentino and Anscoli-Israel 2006). People living in institutions receive less daylight and more night-time light exposure than their counterparts living in the community (Schochat, Martin and Marle 2000). In Chapter 3, on sleep, the importance of increasing residents' day-time exposure to light was stressed. Here the need to reduce the light exposure is emphasised.

People with dementia require very clear information about what they are supposed to be doing, as their own cognitive skills will be impaired and unable to compensate for wrong or misguiding information. It is critical that the brain is given clear cues and clues that the time has come for bed and sleep. Leaving bright lights on does not provide the feeling or recognition of night and bedtime. Lights need to be dimmed so that there is a message that it is time for bed. Once people are in bed, attention should be paid to the amount of light to which they are exposed.

The most problematic area of lighting is the amount of light used when people are being checked. The use of dimmer switches and torches enable staff to light the bedroom slowly when they go in to check rather than using the main light to the room. The main light will flood the room with bright light that is startling and also does not take account of the fact that older people's eyes take longer to adjust to light changes.

There is something of a paradox in relation to lighting at night. On the one hand, people need to have dark rooms to help them sleep and dim lights in the corridors to reduce the light filtering into their rooms. On the other hand, if people are going to find their way to the toilet, the sitting room or indeed any other area at night, then they need very clear light. Older people need twice as much light as younger people and people with dementia need even more (Pollock *et al.* 2008). It is important, therefore, to make sure that the things that people need to see at night are well lit. Make sure that the bathroom door is targeted with light and also that the toilet itself is targeted. It may be important to make sure that the door is open as well as lit. This may not be necessary during the day but it will be important at night. The use of movement-sensitive lighting can help to deal with this. This is lighting that comes on or, if already dimly on, brightens as there is movement towards it. The light will dim or go out once the person has moved on.

For en-suite rooms there may be a conflicting set of needs. The person needs darkness to help them sleep but light to enable them to see the toilet. Movement-sensitive mats may be the answer to this. When the person gets out of bed, the lights will go on and so guide them towards the toilet. Because older people have difficulty with seeing colours clearly at night-time, colour can be diminished. So red may look more like a faded pink. It is important, therefore, that lamps are used that give good colour rendering to maintain the depth of colour that exists in the daylight (Pollock *et al.* 2008).

# Flooring

## CASE STUDY 18

Albert, an 82-year-old man with a diagnosis of dementia, recently moved into a nursing home. One of the reasons he had moved into the home was because he had started to fall at home.

At about 10 p.m. most residents were in bed, but Albert was still up watching a film on the television. The film ended and Albert stood up. He then looked at the floor.

The room had a carpet with large cream circles. Albert bent over, hand cupped in an attempt to pick one of these 'plates' off the floor.

He was caught just before he toppled over.

## CASE STUDY 19

Theresa, a woman in her 90s with a diagnosis of dementia, came out of her room at 2 a.m. She walked along the corridor, apparently in search of the toilet.

Suddenly she stopped and, looking agitated, hovered for a while then turned round and went back the way she came. She was now very agitated and when she got to her room she urinated on the floor.

## CASE STUDY 20

Isobel has an en-suite toilet and bath in her bedroom. She has always been able to use the toilet when she needed to. She has also derived great pleasure from having long leisurely baths. One night as her key worker helped her to the bathroom where she had prepared her bath with bubbles, music and soft lighting, Isobel froze. She refused to go into the bathroom. She actually became quite agitated and gripped the staff member's arm. She shouted and refused to be coaxed into the bathroom.

These case studies are illustrations of three fairly common events. Theresa had a humiliating and upsetting experience, and Albert nearly had a dangerous one. Isobel was agitated, angry and potentially aggressive and was denied the wonderful opportunity to have a relaxing bath.

All of these episodes would have been avoided if attention had been paid to the flooring of the homes. This is, of course, not just a night-time issue, but in all the case studies above it affected people at night.

One of the effects of dementia on the brain is that it damages the parietal lobe. The right-side parietal lobe is our three-dimensional centre. This enables us to see things on different levels. Once this is damaged, our ability to tell if something is flat or not is impaired. This means that people with dementia, with this damage, will see different colours as different levels.

To Albert, the cream circles looked like plates on the carpet. What spooked Theresa was a shadow from a light in the corridor; the dark shadow cast across her path looked like a hole or ditch. The bathroom floor was highly reflective vinyl; to Isobel, the glare caused by the light made the surface look like water.

It is important for night staff to know how flooring might be affecting residents and see how they can combat the negative affects. For example:

- Have lighting that does not throw shadows.
- Where there are differences in carpet colour, try to distract people so that they do not look down. (Better still, approach management and ask for new carpets.)
- There is no longer any need to have the shiny, often flecked, non-slip flooring; there is now dull non-slip flooring available.

Often the solutions are simple. In one home, staff reduced night-time falls for one woman by using a brightly coloured cover over the pressure mat. Previously, the woman had tried to get out of bed by climbing over the bottom in an effort to avoid the dark pressure mat that looked to her like a hole. She saw the brightly coloured cover as a mat and deliberately stepped on to it.

## Signage and colours

It is essential that appropriate signage and colours are used to enable older people and particularly people with dementia to see their environments clearly and to locate themselves within those environments. Changes to the eye mean that older people inhabit a darker and hazier world (Pollock *et al.* 2008). This is because the lens within the ageing eye gradually becomes thicker, less clear, and begins to absorb more blue light, resulting in older people having:

- a dimmer view of their surroundings – a typical 60-year-old person receives about one third of the retinal illuminance of a 20-year-old
- a reduction of contrast in images, leading to difficulties in differentiating subtle changes in the environment such as carpets, stairs, etc.
- a reduction in saturation or vividness of the colours of images – for example, reds begin to look like pinks
- a reduced ability to discriminate blue colours
- an increase in the time needed to adapt to different light levels when moving from one area to another. (Pollock *et al.* 2008, p.12)

Additionally, people with dementia have more difficulty with seeing colours clearly and so certain colours become problematic. It is easier to see primary colours, and generally the colours at the top end of the spectrum rather than those at the bottom. If you think of the colours of the rainbow – red, orange, yellow, green, blue, indigo and violet – then it is more likely that people will see the reds and oranges and yellows. This suggests that if we want people with dementia, and indeed older people generally, to see things, we should use one of the colours at the top end of the spectrum. Paint toilet doors red and people will pick them out more easily. Having red toilet seats is a real aid to enabling people to see and use the toilet better. The important thing is to have a contrast, so if you cannot use red, use some other colours that will highlight the different objects.

Remember also to give visual cues. A picture of a toilet on the toilet door will let people with dementia know what is behind it. They may well know in the day, but increased confusion at night and a decreased ability to orientate themselves may mean that the toilet becomes more difficult to find and recognise. As indicated earlier, it may also be important to highlight the signs on doors at night using directed light. The toilet sign may be in shadow or just too dark to see at night, even though it may be perfectly visible in the day.

# Mirrors

### CASE STUDY 21

The staff supporting Caroline, an 82-year-old woman with a diagnosis of dementia, have asked the doctor to prescribe something to help control her night-time 'hallucinations'. Caroline becomes very, very disturbed at night. She screams that someone is in her bedroom. She often says that 'he is going to rape me'. When staff go into the room, she is shaking and demands they get rid of him.

### CASE STUDY 22

Lizzie, a 78-year-old woman with a diagnosis of dementia, becomes very distressed at night. She shouts that she wants 'them out of here' and 'they are dancing on the end of my bed'. As with Caroline, staff are concerned that Lizzie is hallucinating and so requires antipsychotic medication or sedation at night.

In her bedroom, Caroline had a wardrobe with a mirror in the middle panel in the front. What she could see at night were shadows in the mirror. She interpreted these as someone in her room. Lizzie had a dressing table at the end of her bed. It had a three-panelled mirror on it. The more she waved her arms about and shouted at it, the more the 'people' reflected in it would dance.

These two examples are illustrative of a fairly common occurrence amongst people with dementia. Many people reading this will have had the experience at night of seeing shadows in a bedroom. We know that these are reflections of trees outside or the light shade outlined against the curtains or some other object. The person with dementia may well not know where they are and they may not have the cognitive skills to think, 'I know I am in bed, safe in my bedroom, and the shadows are trees.'

A particular problem for people with dementia is the consequence of losing short-term and longer-term memory. As their memories become more located in a time when they were younger, they will believe themselves to *be* younger. If they have gone back 40 or 50 years, then when they look in the mirror and see an elderly person, they 'know' that it cannot be them as they think that they are now only 20 or 30 years old. The person they see is unknown and an intruder.

It is not hard to imagine how frightening this must be. This is not hallucination; it is a misinterpretation. The easiest solution is simply to cover the mirror. Mirrors can also be a problem during the day and so this may be a problem that needs to be shared with day staff. It may be that day staff do not see or hear people in their bedrooms and so think this is simply a night problem but it is often a greater problem at night. Related to this issue is the need to make sure that curtains are drawn at night. In just the same way as the reflection in the mirror can be misinterpreted, so can the reflection in the window. People may think that intruders are trying to get into their room.

It is worth noting that, as is so often the case with people with dementia, things are not so cut and dried. It sometimes happens that the mirror can be a source of comfort. I once knocked on the bedroom door of a woman with dementia. She invited me in but told me I would need to sit and wait as she was having tea with her mother. She was sitting in front of the mirror on her dressing table with cup and saucer and biscuit. In the mirror she saw an elderly woman. She mistook this reflection for her mother.

## Assistive technology

Assistive technology refers to:

> any device or system that allows an individual to perform a task that they would otherwise be unable to do or increases the ease and safety with which the task can be performed. (Royal Commission on Long Term Care 1999)

The use of technology can raise ethical issues. If devices such as cameras, microphones and global positioning systems (GPS) are being used, there may well be issues around people's privacy and untoward surveillance. The introduction of such devices and systems needs to be given proper consideration and 'best interest' criteria used. There are technologies, however, that are not so intrusive, and where they clearly enable people, increase their independence and even reduce the likelihood of them falling over, they should be considered.

The use of pressure-sensitive mats is a cheap, unobtrusive way to allow staff to monitor people's night-time regimes. For safety reasons, the mat should always be under the carpet. If staff know people's night-time routine – for example, how long they usually take to go to the toilet – they can use the information from the mat to let them know when people get out of bed and when they return. Staff need only respond if the return is delayed.

Woods and Ashley (1995) used an environmental intervention known as Simulation Presences Therapy (SPT) and reported it was successful in alleviating difficult behaviours such as social isolation, verbal aggression or agitation. The purpose of SPT is to provide a personalised intervention for people with moderate to severe dementia. An example of the therapy would be the use of some pleasant and reassuring memories in the form of a telephone conversation using a continuous-play audio-tape system. The person, on lifting the phone and dialling, would hear a voice, perhaps a family member's voice if appropriate, which would provide calming talk. The intervention can be used for extended periods of time because each repetition is viewed as a fresh, live telephone call. At night, when people can become worried and mull over sad memories, this could be a very useful intervention. There is, of course, the possibility that this might be disconcerting and so distress the person. As with all interventions, decisions have to be made on an individual basis.

The use of verbal interventions can also reduce agitation and 'wandering' at night if, for example, they enable people to return to bed after going to the toilet. A verbal reminder, triggered by breaking an infrared beam, that tells people that it is the middle of the night and they need to return to bed and not go to the kitchen can be reassuring. It may also be reassuring if the voice is of a person familiar to the person with dementia. This type of technology is not expensive to install and can, as long as the person is not frightened by the disembodied voice, be a useful addition to the environment.

There are many environmental issues that need to be considered to support older people who are frail, visually or hearing impaired, or have dementia, throughout the 24 hours of care. There are, however, some environmental considerations that are particularly important to consider at night. Few of the above cost much but can be critical to the development of suitable night care.

## Summary

During the night the needs of the residents have to be balanced with the needs of the staff to undertake their caring duties: for staff, the home is a place of work in which they have to be alert, organised, responsible and mobile; for residents, the night is essentially about sleep, rest, little or no activity and a great deal of dependence.

The competing needs of the two groups places demands on the environment of the home during the night that are different from those of the day. The night-time environment, therefore, needs to be considered separately from the daytime environment. Issues such as noise and light levels, flooring, signage, colour, mirrors and assistive technology need to be given a night-time perspective.

Most of the environmental requirements proposed in this chapter are not expensive (in fact, many are free) or complicated to put in place, and yet they can make a dramatic difference to the night-time experiences and quality of life of residents. They make the environment more conducive to sleep, enable residents to have more control at night and may well reduce the incidence of falls.

Chapter 9

# Night-Time Activities

## CASE STUDY 23

Mr Phillips spends a large part of every night awake. He will go to bed at 10 p.m., go into a deep sleep and then wake at 2 a.m. He is then unable to sleep again until about 4 a.m. This has been his pattern for many years. His wife says that often he would get up, go downstairs to the sitting room and listen to the World Service on the radio.

When they find him walking down the corridor at 2 o'clock in the morning, the staff will steer him back to bed and suggest he tries to get some sleep.

He often appears again in the corridor within minutes. The staff think he would benefit from some sedation. Mrs Phillips does not agree!

When one of the stated tasks of night staff is to 'promote sleep', it may seem to be a bit strange to have this section in this book. We are not suggesting that staff set up activities for residents. What is needed is for night staff to 'go with the flow' when people wake at night. Sometimes they will just want company, sometimes they will want food and/or a drink and sometimes they will want to do something.

For some people, the need to have something to eat is an activity in its own right. This has been covered in Chapter 7, but in the context of this section it can be seen not just as a matter of nutrition but also as a comforting and social activity. A common activity for many people, not just older people, is to listen to the radio at night. Some people will leave the radio on all night as a comfort. Others will want to turn it on when they are lying awake in the middle of the night. The BBC World Service can provide hours of interest throughout the night. However, this can also be a source of agitation as people hear about world events and news and then have difficulty sleeping. It is worth checking if people have been World Service listeners prior to coming into care home settings. For someone having difficulty sleeping, the opportunity to have a cup of tea with a good radio play could be very comforting and remove some of the anxiety that the night can bring.

This might, however, be too stimulating and the opportunity to simply lie and listen to soothing music may be a suitable and rewarding night-time activity. The leaflet in Figure 9.1 was developed by a social care and leisure manager for night staff working in a nursing home. The intention is to make this information available, probably on a notice board, so that any night staff could access calm soothing music throughout the night for people who wake and cannot return easily to sleep.

Night staff care for people from mid-evening onwards. The time after the evening meal and before bedtime is often a time when people in their daily lives take up many different activities. Before entering the home, people may well have had evening routines that involved a number of activities such as preparing for the next day, knitting, doing housework, playing cards, visiting friends, reading, doing the crossword, being on the computer, reading the paper or phoning friends.

Unfortunately, where there are activities coordinators in a care home, they usually leave at the end of the working day. This is partly because of the needs of the worker but also because it is, erroneously, assumed that people in care homes are too tired by the evening to undertake any meaningful activity. This is a great shame. Some people are undoubtedly tired and ready for bed; for others, 'going to bed' too easily becomes the evening's activity.

CALM & GENTLE NIGHTS BY THE RADIO

Relaxing Classics 11PM CLASSIC FM

99.9–101.9 FM classicfm.com


Through the Night 1AM BBC RADIO 3

90.2–92.4 FM bbc.co.uk/radio3

Figure 9.1 Night-time radio information leaflet for staff (Thanks to Annabelle Meredith 2009)

For many, however, an activity can perk them up and this will in turn make it more likely that they will sleep better when they do eventually go to bed.

There are a number of suitable activities for the night-time. The following are simply a few suggestions. You will know your residents best and will know which activities suit which people and be able to adjust them accordingly.

## A walk in the evening air

The authors of this book live in Scotland. Here, as in all northern hemisphere countries, the summer evenings are light, often in the furthest northern areas until 11 p.m. It is frustrating to see (and probably frustrating to experience) people sitting indoors at such times. An early evening stroll round the gardens or even sitting watching the sun go down would provide a meaningful and stimulating activity. It may well replicate one that people engaged in earlier in their life.

## Life story work

Life story work is an intervention that involves the recording and sharing of a person's past. It is important for all of us to hang on to our past, our memories and the things that made us who we are. For people without dementia, this can more easily be accessed and understood. For people with dementia, it is even more important that staff know about the person's past. This activity may have been developed by day staff. The person's life story can be collated and recorded in books, on a computer and in boxes. If life story work has been carried out, night staff will not only be better able to understand the person but will also be better able to develop suitable, failure-free, person-centred activities.

As dementia progresses, it can be hard to find suitable failure-free activities that will not cause stress. Life story work, as long as only positive memories are recorded, can provide a suitable failure-free activity. The focus on the past also encourages staff to attend to people's need to reminisce. With the progression of a dementia, previous activities will become problematic for people. The need to develop stress- and failure-free activities should be the focus of activity-based interventions. The use of life story work that does not focus on past painful, unhappy experiences and memories fits the bill perfectly. People are able to access objects and stories that have meaning and give pleasure.

## Developing life story work

Developing life stories involves a series of activities that will probably result in the production of a book and/or a box of memorabilia, but this is not the focus of the work. It is important to see this as a work in progress and not focus on the end product. The process of talking to people about their memories and collecting objects and pictures should be treated as an activity in its own right. The use of a box of objects and stories can be very powerful. A box allows people to see things clearly. Importantly, it also means that objects that they like to touch are easily available. Objects from their past that hold important memories can more easily be accessed by having them there to hold. The use of important and well-known music from the past can be evocative and provide a source for reminiscence and stories. Be as imaginative as you can about the possible contents of the box.

It is important to leave the work in an accessible place with the proviso that confidentiality and the protection of the contents is maintained. Remember also that the life story materials belong to the person and no one else has right of access. This fact was underlined by a story box which had the following paragraph attached:

This is my life story box.

I don't mind you looking through the box at the 'memories' that make up my life as long as you ask permission first and also that you take care, as it is very special to me. I would like you to look at my life story work and talk with me about all the memories in it. Please remember that this box contains a lot of private and personal memories to me and should be treated with respect at all times. Thank you.

Night staff can use various objects and information to develop activities either for individuals or for small groups with similar interests and memories.

## A visit from a minister of religion

### CASE STUDY 24

The Reverend Anderson made a point of visiting his parishioners who lived in care homes during the evenings. His reason was that it was in the hours of the night that people often wanted solace. People seemed to value his presence before going to bed. His calm presence also seemed to give comfort. It was also a relatively quiet time when he could more easily engage with people.

For many older people, the time before bed was when they said their prayers and the Reverend was able to engage in this act of worship with them.

This is a meaningful and spiritually rewarding activity. It also means that someone else is in the home during the early night-time.

## Having a snack

In all homes people will be offered a nightcap before they go to bed. This activity is not only comforting but also signals the change in the evening activity. It is a way of steering people towards bedtime.

It is important, however, to recognise that for some people there may also be a desire to eat during the night. Some people, prior to going into a home, will have got up and had a snack during the night. People who were night workers may very well have acquired a habit of eating in the middle of the night. Night staff will no doubt understand this, as this will be their own experience. Bell *et al.* comment that:

> there is something wonderful about a late night snack. It's a guilty pleasure. When persons with dementia stay up late or get up during the night, sometimes a small snack (including one shared with a caregiver) can become a focal point of an activity and provide a comforting feeling of home. (2004, p.192)

It is important to have suitable food available, of course. This is dealt with in more detail in Chapter 7 on night-time nutrition.

It is also worth noting that people with dementia particularly need calm, failure-free environments, preferably with one-to-one support to help with their eating. Night-time better replicates this than the busy day, and night staff could capitalise on this to enable people to have a more enjoyable, less stressful eating activity.

## After dinner activities

Bell *et al.* (2004) have identified a number of what they call 'after dinner activities'. Interestingly, all the activities they identify require that life story work has already been developed. If person-centred, meaningful activities are going to be developed, then it is important to know about the person's past likes, dislikes, hobbies, activities and experiences.

In Figure 9.2 we have provided two examples of 'after dinner activities' – reading aloud and sing-along – from their book *The Best Friends Book of Alzheimer's Activities*. To demonstrate the many levels on which the activity can be meaningful, enjoyable and person-centred, Bell *et al.* emphasise certain areas such as humour, spirituality and music, and show how the activity links with the different areas. It provides a convincing reason for doing the activity and begs the question 'why not?' The book is an American publication. It may be that some things need to be adapted to suit different cultures. It is also important to emphasise that the activities are generally described for the period after dinner. This does not necessarily mean that such a restriction should be maintained. Later in the evening, even quite late on, these activities could be used. On an individual level they could, and perhaps should, be used through the night, as appropriate.

*Reading aloud*

Many of us have fond memories of being read to as children or reading aloud to our own children. *Persons* with dementia can often read aloud very well even when they are having trouble with conversation.

## The Basics

Build a collection of reading-aloud materials. Choose familiar readings, prayers, poems, and jokes.

Find a place for a small group to meet. It is important to meet in the same place and at the same time. Decide on a name for the group, such as Study Group or Book Club. This can be an individual activity in the home or a residential setting

Consider some bedside reading with a *person* to evoke nostalgic memories and help them go to sleep.

## The Best Friends Way

**Life Story**: Take note of those who have an interest in reading of any kind. Have *persons* been teachers, worked in a library, or read to children and grandchildren?

**Humor**: There are funny joke books, misquotes in newsletters and newspapers, and many humorous poems and stories.

**Early Dementia**: *Persons* often can read exceedingly well. They should be encouraged to read aloud to the group.

**Late Dementia**: *Persons* in late dementia can respond to very familiar prayers, readings and childhood rhymes. They should be encouraged to be part of the group if they seem to enjoy it.

**Music**: Reading lyrics from familiar songs can prompt *persons* to break into song.

**Old Skills**: Reading aloud is an old skill, fine-tuned through the years, and is often intact far into the disease.

**Sensory**: The rhythmic tone of being read to can be calming and reassuring.

**Spirituality**: *Persons* can be connected to their particular religious or spiritual quest by hearing meaningful selections read aloud to them.

**Conversation**: Celebrate, "We have this nice place for our reading group and lots of interesting material to read." Compliment, "Myrtle, I know you have spent many hours reading stories to be recorded for the blind. That was a wonderful contribution" or "Nellie, I love your reading style." Ask for an opinion, "Mark, I know you taught ancient literature. Did you have a favorite fable?"

*Sing-Along*

Human beings are made to sing. *Persons with dementia can recall the words of familiar songs and delight in having an opportunity to sing, making this a favorite evening activity.*

## The Basics

Create your own, large-type songbooks with lyrics from familiar songs. It's always good to look for a volunteer or staff member to be a pianist, guitarist, or other musical accompanist, but sing-along tapes are available.

Be consistent. Meet in the same location at the same time (just after dinner if possible), and have a defined length of time for singing, such as 30 minutes. Decide on a name for the group such as "The Song Birds." Arrange the seating in a semicircle around the accompanist. It is fun to have a theme song to begin and a favorite song for the ending. Enjoy hymns or religious music now and then, but be sensitive to persons who come from different backgrounds. This activity can be done any time, but for nighttime, slow down the pace.

## The Best Friends Way

**Life Story**: Did anyone sing together as a family around the piano when they were growing up? Are there choir members from hometown churches, communities, or schools? Was anyone a professional singer? Who sang in the shower?

**The Arts**: Change the names in some songs to include members of the group, such as changing the name "Good Night Irene" to Matthew or Corrine. Write new verses to some songs.

**Exercise**: Singing is good for deep breathing and is relaxing at the end of the day.

**Humor**: Talk and laugh about not being able to carry a tune. Sing some funny songs and keep the sing-along light hearted and fun.

**Early Dementia**: *Persons* may be able to play the piano or guitar, call out the number of the page of each song, or lead the singing.

**Old Skills**: Singing is an old skill, and even those who are nonverbal in conversation can often sing every word to a familiar song.

**Sensory**: Hearing the tones, feeling the rhythm and seeing the facial expressions of the singers all excite the senses.

**Conversation**: Use the life story, "Lottie, let's sing your favorite song, 'Let Me Call You Sweetheart.' I like that one too." Compliment, "Mark, I like to sing next to you. You help me stay in tune." Reminisce, "Did your mother sing songs to you at bedtime when you were a little boy?" Ponder after singing the song, "What is a tootsie wootsie?"

Figure 9.2 Two examples of 'after dinner activities'
*Source*: Bell *et al.* (1994) The Best Friends Book of Alzheimer's Activities, Volume One. Baltimore: Health Professions Press, Inc. Reprinted by permission.

Finally, make sure that there is a gently lit space at night for people to sit in with memory boxes, magazines and books around to provide failure-free, familiar activity. It is, of course, important that staff are alert to the fact that people may need a good reading light as well as the gentle night-light.

The use of recliner chairs for people at night can facilitate relaxation. The provision of throws and cushions may enable people to relax and feel more 'at home' during the night.

These ideas provide opportunities for people to stay up for a while and not be or feel pressured into going back to bed.

This does, of course, cause a potential pressure for staff. If there are only two or three staff on duty for 30 or 40 people, then attending to people sitting in a quiet room takes them away from other essential tasks. Unfortunately, this 'need' for night-time activity is not usually factored in to calculations about staffing levels at night.

## Summary

When one of the stated tasks of night staff is to 'promote sleep', it may seem to be a bit strange to have this section in this book. We are not suggesting that staff set up activities for residents. What is needed is for night staff to 'go with the flow' when people wake at night. Residents who wake at night will do so for a variety of reasons. Sometimes they will just want company, sometimes they will want food and/or a drink and sometimes they will want to do something.

This section has explored the appropriate use of activity throughout the night, starting with after-dinner activities through to calmer, quieter, usually more individual activities in the middle of the night. The use of evening strolls in the garden, reading aloud, visits from religious representatives, the use of life story work and the employment of late-night music programmes on the radio are some of the suggestions given.

A gently lit space at night will enable people to sit with memory boxes, magazines and books which will provide failure-free, familiar activity. The use of recliner chairs for people at night can enable residents to be up but relaxed.

Chapter 10

# Responding to the Pain Experiences of People at Night

## CASE STUDY 25

Jack, a man with dementia, had been a professional footballer in his youth. He has severe arthritic pain in his knees as a consequence.

During the day staff would sometimes give him pain relief as they saw him walking at a snail's pace along the corridor. It was clear that he was in great pain with his knees.

At night Jack would groan and be uncharacteristically verbally aggressive towards staff. He slept very little and complained of his lumpy mattress and was seen as 'a real old moan' by the night staff. In the mornings he was particularly 'stubborn' and 'aggressive'.

Jack was clearly in a lot of pain. Arthritic joints do not stop hurting at night. It is just that people are not so obviously struggling to do various activities. Throughout the night Jack would toss and turn on what he described as a lumpy mattress. It was his way of saying that it hurt. Arthritic joints seize up through the night and are particularly stiff and sore in the morning.

As with most of the other topics in this book, much that is contained within this chapter is relevant to day as well as night staff. There are, however, some aspects that are more relevant to night staff and these will be highlighted. As people age they will develop the conditions of older age. These often lead to higher levels of disability and a greater incidence of physical pain (Main and Spanswick 2000). Conditions such as degenerative joint disease, arthritis, osteoporosis and Parkinson's disease will increase the likelihood of older people experiencing both acute and persistent chronic pain. It has been estimated that in any four-week period 64–86 per cent of older people will suffer with chronic pain (Tsai and Chang 2004).

The existence of pain can cause a number of other experiences and conditions that further diminish the well-being and ability to cope. Jones *et al.* (2004) found the following consequences of poorly or untreated pain:

- anxiety and agitation
- physical dysfunction
- sleep disturbance
- poor nutrition
- delayed healing
- decreased activity
- depression.

McCracken and Iverson (2001) found that chronic pain can have a negative effect on cognitive function, resulting in forgetfulness, minor accidents, difficulty finishing tasks and attention difficulties. One of the dangers is that if the cause of the above changes is not linked to pain, then people may well be given inappropriate medication that does not deal with the underlying problem. They are left still in pain. In a care home for older people there is going to be a high level of pain experienced by residents. One study in Australia (McClean and Higginbotham 2002) found that at any one time 28 per cent of residents were in pain, and that women reported more pain than men (31% compared to 21%). The pain was found mostly in limbs, joints and back.

Staff awareness of people's pain experiences is crucial if there is going to be an appropriate diagnosis and effective pain relief. There are, however, a number of problems that surround pain recognition amongst older people generally and people with dementia in particular. Many older people are reluctant to acknowledge their pain. McClean (2000) elicited the following responses and reasons for this reluctance:

- fear of painful investigation
- denial: 'If I ignore the pain it will go away'
- 'I don't want to lose control in making decisions about my body'
- 'I don't want to bother other people'
- 'I don't want to be thought of as a complainer'
- 'I may be given drugs that will make me an addict'.

In one study of 148 patients it was found that:

- 11 per cent viewed suffering as a challenge with positive effects
- 13 per cent viewed pain as a punishment for some wrong deed
- 10 per cent of patients rarely complained because they thought it was a sign of weakness. (McClean 2000)

People with dementia are equally at risk of having painful conditions as the general older population (Horgas and Elliott 2001), yet they receive even less pain relief than older people without dementia (Horgas and Tsai 1998). The more disorientated they are, the less pain relief they receive (Horgas and Tsai 1998), resulting in some examples of unacceptable practices such as the following:

- Even when analgesia is prescribed to people with dementia, 83 per cent do not receive their medication (Dawson 1998).

- Seventy-six per cent of people with dementia did not receive regular analgesia post operative hip repair, despite 42 per cent expected to be in severe pain (Morrison and Sui 2000).

Why is pain relief for people with dementia more problematic than for the general population?

## Communication difficulties associated with dementia

Pain is a highly subjective experience. Many things will influence how an individual will experience pain: culture, age, ethnicity and gender are the main variables. The person with pain is the only person who knows how severe and enduring the pain is. It may feel worse at night when the person is alone and more likely to worry. One useful definition is that 'pain is whatever the patient says it is, and occurs whenever the patient says it does' (McCaffery 1968, p.95). This presents problems for pain identification in relation to people with dementia where communication is an increasing problem.

People with dementia will start to lose the words they might have had to describe pain. As described in Chapter 4, damage to the parietal lobes results in a number of significant problems for pain communication. Amongst other things, the left side parietal lobe is responsible for our understanding of patterns, essential for the use of language where the patterning of words is critical to communication. The left side lobe is also responsible for our understanding of the patterns and geography of our body: it tells us which is our right and which is our left side. Once the part of the brain that tells people where their head, their foot, their left and their right are becomes damaged, then they can no longer physically indicate where the pain is located. The person with a toothache may not only fail to find the word 'toothache'; she may also be unable to locate the place where the pain is and will not be able to put her hand there.

People will sometimes use a general phase such as 'my head hurts' because they cannot find the word 'toothache', but they are communicating that there is a pain. This can lead to problems for assessment. If someone persistently says her leg hurts and yet she is walking well, there is a temptation to think that there is no pain and that the person wants attention. It may be that the pain is elsewhere.

People will often use phrases they used in the past as a generalised way of expressing pain. For example, people may constantly say they have a 'tummy ache'. This does not mean that this is the location of the pain; it is simply the use of a well-remembered pain-related phrase. Perhaps this was a pain they would have had in their childhood and probably the one best remembered. 'I can't go to school, I have a tummy ache' might be a phrase that was well used when they were young. Or they will remember their parents saying, 'what is wrong, have you got a tummy ache?' The person may use a phrase as a substitute for the correct word: 'oh dear, oh dear' will indicate distress but there may be a failure to recognise this as an expression of physical rather than emotional pain. The person may not be able to use any words but may shout or groan. Sometimes the communication will not be through words at all but through actions. These actions, such as pacing and head-banging, may be seen as 'challenging behaviour'.

Staff have to ascertain the nature of the pain through observation and communication. The need to pay attention to subtle and often almost imperceptible changes is critical. The key to pain recognition may be the look of 'worried eyes' or the slight change in pallor or shifting movements.

## Diagnostic overshadowing

Diagnostic overshadowing occurs when a diagnosis for one illness or condition becomes the explanation for all subsequent changes in the person's health and behaviour.

It is recognised that within the general population of people with dementia there is a tendency to attribute changes in the individual to the progression of their dementia, rather than other causes (Mason and Scior 2004).

People with dementia tend to wake at night more frequently than people without dementia. This is partly the result of changes to their circadian rhythm. There is, as a result, a tendency amongst those supporting people with dementia to attribute all night-time disturbances to the impact of the dementia. However, there are many non-dementia-related reasons why someone may wake at night. The existence of painful conditions is one of these.

One of the painful conditions that many older people experience is arthritis, which is particularly painful at night when joints stiffen. Jack, who features at the beginning of this chapter, is fairly typical of the type of experience people will have. Throughout the night people with conditions such as arthritis will experience joint pain. In the morning they will be stiff and movement will be painful.

## Pain as a cause of challenging behaviour

Staff working with people with dementia often experience 'challenging behaviour'. Training courses on dementia will usually consider and focus on the prevention, causes and management of 'challenging behaviour'. This is essential knowledge but it can have the undesired effect of staff mistakenly seeing challenging behaviour rather than pain.

Pain is positively associated with screaming, aggression and verbal agitation in dementia (Cohen-Mansfield, Werner and Marx 1990). When thinking about what types of behaviours can result from pain experiences, questionnaires to groups of staff highlighted most of the following:

- increased irritation
- moaning
- withdrawal
- crying
- screaming
- swearing
- aggression
- poor eating
- anxiety
- hitting out if touched or threatened to be touched in the painful area.

Many of these behaviours are also those labelled as challenging amongst people who have dementia. The case study below provides a good example of the way in which pain-related behaviour might be misinterpreted.

## CASE STUDY 26

Adele was a gentle woman whom day staff found charming and compliant. Night staff, however, found her to be verbally aggressive. At night she would wake and shout out to people when they came into her room. This was particularly the case if staff changed her incontinence pad. In the mornings she was very 'uncooperative'. She would refuse to get out of bed. As staff tried to dress her she would shout and sometimes hit out at them. Adele had arthritis.

After the night staff were given training on pain relief, Adele was given two paracetamol 20 minutes before she got up. She would rise more easily and the 'challenging behaviour' disappeared.

This is an example of an alternative response to 'challenging behaviour'. Give pain relief and see if the behaviour changes. If it does, then the person's behaviour will change and this will be an indication that the behaviour is caused by pain. The next stage is to identify where the pain is and what is causing it. The use of pain relief can begin the process of proper diagnosis.

## The use of 'as required' (PRN) medication

### CASE STUDY 27

Mrs Fraser is aged 93 and diagnosed with Alzheimer's type dementia. She had poor sleep and was very unsettled at night. She called out, banged the walls and paged the staff constantly. When staff attended to her, she was unsure what assistance she wanted. Ongoing reassurance from staff made no difference. After training on pain and dementia the night staff approached the GP and asked to have Mrs Fraser's pain relief and night sedation reviewed. Pain relief was moved from 'as required' to 'regular' administration. Night sedation was reduced.

Mrs Fraser is now getting five hours' uninterrupted sleep each night, albeit from 2 a.m. onwards. She has become more settled and 'happier within herself' and her mobility has improved.

Pain relief is often prescribed 'as required' or PRN. McClean and Cunningham (2007) comment that some people might think this stands for 'Pain Relief Never', and for people with dementia this practice is problematic. If, as indicated above, people supporting the person with dementia do not know when the person is in pain, then how can they be certain that they know when it is 'required'? There is evidence that for people with dementia there is not only less prescribing of analgesia than amongst an age-matched population without dementia, but even when analgesia is prescribed to people with dementia, 83 per cent do not receive it (Dawson 1998).

The World Health Organization (WHO) guidelines on prescribing analgesia to people with dementia are clear: 'as required' should not be the primary approach to pain management for people with dementia. There should be regular administration; the treatment should be adjusted from one step to the next according to increasing or decreasing pain severity, history of response and side-effect profile (WHO 1996).

It is important that once analgesia is given, there is a monitoring process. Someone in a care home will have a number of people caring for them throughout the 24 hours of the day. One member of staff may give pain relief and by the time the effects have worn off someone else may be on duty. All staff involved should know about the pain relief given and should monitor and evaluate it. There may be a tendency amongst some people who have a reluctance to use drugs to under-treat. This is not an option if the pain relief is going to be properly administered and monitored. There are a number of options that need to be considered in the administration of pain relief.

## CASE STUDY 28

Mrs Perry, a woman in her late 80s with a diagnosis of dementia, had a large hernia. This clearly caused her pain and kept her awake and distressed at night. She had paracetomol prescribed 'as required'.

Training for night staff on pain relief and the introduction of a new practice surgery led to a review of Mrs Perry's medication and in particular of her pain relief. Regular pain relief was prescribed. Mrs Perry had difficulty swallowing and so, quite understandably, refused the tablets (bringing into question how often she received the 'as required' medication if she was unable to take tablets). Liquid medication worked sometimes but not every time. The decision was made to use transdermal patches. Both night and day staff noticed 'very positive' results. Mrs Perry became much less distressed and had noticeably improved sleep.

For people with problems swallowing, the use of liquid pain relief or transdermal patches may remove some of the distress a person with dementia may have when needing to take regular pain relief. This may also be helpful to people without dementia who might have problems with swallowing.

Patches may not be suitable for everyone. The presence of certain illnesses and conditions or the use of other medications may be counter-indicative. This is something that the GP will be able to advise on. When the first patch is used, it may take up to three days for the maximum effect to be experienced. The person may need some other painkillers in the interim.

## Non-pharmaceutical interventions to relieve pain

Non-pharmaceutical interventions can prevent, reduce and relieve. For chronic musculoskeletal pain which is associated with increased age, the application of heat and massage or positioning can sometimes be all that is needed (McClean 2000). Chronic degenerative joint disease causes pain in the back and limbs; ostoeporotic spinal deformity also causes back pain. The need to support people's bodies with appropriate seating, the use of aromatherapy, massage and music to relax people, and the slowing down of activities and interventions will all contribute to pain reduction. People in pain will tense up and stiffen their body. The significance of almost all the above interventions is that they are directly or indirectly relaxing. They do not necessarily take the pain away but they may reduce the secondary impact and so may make it more tolerable.

> There is research that shows that the very presence of a caring nurse in close proximity to a patient leads to a significant reduction in perceived pain intensity, even though the nurse does not administer any treatment. (McClean and Cunningham 2007, p.25)

The use of some of these interventions at night, especially aromatherapy, could help people to sleep better. A number of these interventions involve touch. People with dementia need to experience touch, both as a form of communication and as a source of comfort (Goldsmith 1996). People in pain can be relieved of pain or at least enabled to cope with it through the appropriate use of touch.

## What do night staff need to do?

Much of what has been written above is equally applicable to day and night staff, but there are some things that deserve particular attention by night staff. Simple changes such as giving pain relief to people with arthritis before they experience the pain of moving and dressing in the morning may make all the difference. Giving people pain relief before they go to bed and then through the night as appropriate will help them to sleep better.

It is equally important to give time to people. Sitting quietly with a cup of tea, showing warmth and touching them in a caring way may reduce pain intensity. Night-time is so much quieter than the day. Staff should use this to give people in pain the calm space they need.

It is important that when people wake at night it is not automatically considered to be an aspect of their dementia. Night staff need to record the times and patterns of waking but also what people say, how they look and walk. This will give clues to the night pain that is being experienced.

Having a pain management strategy in place is essential and this requires a team approach. Night staff must communicate well with day staff about people's pain levels and needs. It may well be that day staff have a different experience and understanding of a resident's pain. There also needs to be a consistent and routine use of a pain assessment tool that will enable staff to systematically record someone's behaviour and pain needs. Kerr *et al.* (2008), however, found that staff rarely used any pain assessment tool.

For many staff the time that it takes to complete assessment tools made the use of any tool unattractive and burdensome. Staff need to be trained to use a suitable tool. However, vital signs of distress and pain may be missed if changes are not recorded.

There are many tools to choose from. A few examples are:

- the Abbey Pain Scale (Abbey *et al.* 2004)
- the Non-communicative Patient's Pain Assessment Instrument (NOPAIN) – this tool focuses on noises, movements and words (http://nursinghomes.tmf. org/Portals/16/Documents/NH/Toolkits/Pain/ PainMgmtpad.pdf)
- the assessment of discomfort in dementia (ADD) protocol (http://prc.coh.org/PainNOA/ADD_B.pdf)
- DOLOPLUS 2 – a French tool developed for the multidimensional assessment of pain in non-verbal elders (www.Doloplus-2.com)
- DISDAT (www.disdat.co.uk).

The assessment and management of pain is a very complex process and it is difficult to recommend any one tool (Herr, Bjoro and Decker 2006; Horgas *et al.* 2007). Finding a tool that staff find useful and easy to complete is part of a fundamental process in providing good care.

The chart in Figure 10.1, which was developed at the University of Stirling, is a tool that should be used by the whole team caring for the older person to determine the probable and possible explanations for changes to behaviour. It also sets out some clear recommended strategies for dealing with the behaviour. It will help staff to answer the question 'What if it's Pain?' It would be a good idea to copy this chart and place it in the staff room and other places that will remind staff to 'think about pain'.

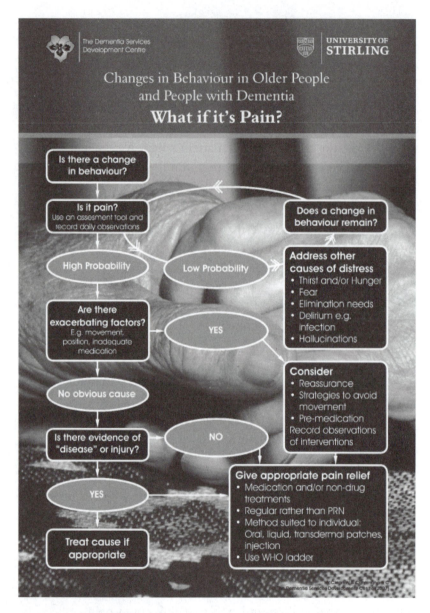

Figure 10.1 Pain and changes in behaviour (Dementia Services Development Centre, University of Stirling 2007)

# Summary

Older people experience a greater incidence of acute and chronic physical pain than younger adults. It has been estimated that in any four-week period 64–86 per cent of older people will suffer with chronic pain (Tsai and Chang 2004). The pain is associated with a variety of age-related conditions such as degenerative joint disease, arthritis, osteoporosis and Parkinson's disease. Many painful conditions will worsen at night.

Night staff awareness of people's pain experiences is crucial if there is going to be an appropriate diagnosis and effective pain relief. There are, however, problems that surround pain recognition amongst older people generally and people with dementia in particular. People with dementia will start to lose the words they might have had to describe pain and may also be unable to locate the place where the pain is. Sometimes the communication will not be through words at all but through actions. These actions may be seen as 'challenging behaviour'. There is then a danger that inappropriate medication is given instead of pain relief.

When pain relief is prescribed to people with dementia, the World Health Organization (WHO) guidelines recommend that 'as required' should not be the primary approach but that regular administration and monitoring should be in place. The use of liquid pain relief or transdermal patches may remove some of the distress a person with dementia may have when needing to take regular pain relief. This may also be helpful to people without dementia who might also have problems with swallowing.

Non-pharmaceutical interventions can prevent, reduce and relieve pain. The need to support people's bodies with appropriate seating, the use of aromatherapy, massage and music for relaxation and the slowing down of activities and interventions will all contribute to pain reduction.

# Chapter 11

# Medication and Night-Time Care

## CASE STUDY 29

Bill is a 78-year-old man with a diagnosis of dementia. He had been living in the nursing home for six months prior to the following events. Bill started to get up frequently through the night. He would become very aggressive towards any member of staff who suggested he return to bed. He was particularly aggressive towards the women. Day staff reported that they considered Bill to be a mild-natured and compliant man. This was not the experience of the night staff.

Bill's shouting and banging disturbed other residents and a decision was made to give him quetiapine, an anti psychotic drug which has a side effect of acting as a sedative. Bill started to sleep longer and became less aggressive when he was awake.

However, Bill then developed lethargy during the day, had a tremor and appeared less motivated generally. He also began to put on weight.

At no point did anyone try to work out what was causing Bill's night-time behaviour.

It is not within the remit of this book to provide detailed information on medication, its uses, impact and efficacy. It is important, however, that all staff looking after people with dementia have some knowledge of the benefits and side effects of medication. Often side effects don't develop until such drugs have been prescribed for some time, and so are not recognised as being side effects. This particularly applies to Parkinson's disease-like symptoms such as tremor and more importantly stiffness and difficulty in moving, and to akathasia (see below). By being better informed it is hoped that staff will be better able to recognise some of the negative effects of medication and will also be better able to discuss their concerns about some prescribing regimes.

Many older people will be taking more than one form of medication. The onset of conditions of older age mean that people's use of medication often increases. People may well be taking a number of different medications at the same time. If this is not closely monitored, there is an increased possibility of an adverse reaction, either to a new drug or to the impact of the polypharmacy, where several different drugs are taken in combination. Medication needs to be reviewed on a regular basis to avoid unwanted side effects from drug interactions (Livingston 2003).

The impact of such polypharmacy can lead to the development of an acute confusional state or delirium. This may mimic the various characteristics of dementia and may lead staff to think that someone's dementia is developing more quickly or that someone without a dementia has suddenly developed the condition. It is essential that staff take note of any such changes and report these to the relevant medical practitioner. It can also be the case that as a result of the changes in metabolism brought about by the ageing process, drugs that people had previously taken and tolerated may begin to cause adverse effects. It is important not to assume that problems with tolerance are necessarily linked to the most recently prescribed medication.

## The use of medication with people with dementia

People with dementia will often exhibit behavioural and psychological problems such as agitation, aggression, wandering, shouting, repeated questioning and sleep disturbance. Too often the answer to these presenting problems is the use of antipsychotic medication such as haloperidol, risperidone, quetiapine or olanzapine. Often they are used for their sedative side effects to manage sleep disturbance and in the management of behaviour that is found challenging.

There has long been concern over the way antipsychotic drugs are often used (and misused), particularly in relation to people with dementia (Hopker 1999; McGrath and Jackson 1997). These drugs can cause increased cognitive decline and confusion. Some will induce akathisia, a frequent and common side effect of antipsychotic drugs. This consists of a feeling of restlessness and the need to keep moving. People may also rock whilst sitting or standing, and lift their feet as if they are marching on the spot, or may cross and uncross their legs whilst sitting. The drugs might also cause drug-induced Parkinson's disease-like symptoms. This may even lead to further medication to counteract the side effects of the primary drug, adding to polypharmacy.

Increasingly, more serious consequences of the use of inappropriate antipsychotic medication in the care of older people, and in particular in relation to people with dementia, are being recognised. Various work has shown that use of two drugs in particular, olanzapine and risperidone, significantly increase the risk of stroke. In the UK in 2004 the Committee for Safety in Medicines issued a caution warning against using these drugs in people with dementia. Similar warnings have been issued in other parts of the world. Subsequent studies have also shown similar problems with other antipsychotics.

There is a particular area of concern in relation to people with Lewy body type dementia. People with this type of dementia will have a serious and potentially life threatening reaction to antipsychotic medications such as haloperidol, fluphenazine and chlorpromazine (McKeith et al. 2004). Generally there will be a worsening of symptoms, extreme muscular rigidity, catatonia, falls, and the development of neuroleptic malignant syndrome which can present a threefold risk of death.

In a study commissioned by the Department of Health, Professor Sube Bannerjee (2009) found after a review of research evidence that antipsychotic medication is still frequently used to manage many of the psychological and behavioural symptoms that are associated with dementia. Along with aggression, agitation and shouting, the medication is also used to treat sleep disturbance. Concern about the overuse and misuse of these drugs was highlighted by Professor Banerjee in his report in which he found that these drugs appeared to have only a limited positive effect in treating these symptoms and further that they can cause harm.

Banerjee estimated that each year 180,000 people with dementia receive antipsychotics in England. Of these, up to 36,000 people benefit to some degree from the treatment. However, around 1620 additional cerebrovascular adverse events (such as stroke) result from the treatment, and about half of these will be severe. It is estimated that approximately 1800 additional deaths each year will be caused by such treatment in this frail population.

Although in some cases – for example, specific subgroups of people with dementia and those with severe symptoms – the drugs may have a beneficial effect, for others they are clearly inappropriate and potentially harmful.

The report estimated that the use of antipsychotic medication could be reduced to a third of current usage over the following three years. This could be achieved by training carers and medical staff to use alternative medications and by increasing the awareness and use of non-pharmaceutical interventions.

Amongst the recommendations the report states that:

- Care homes should be assessed based on their use of antipsychotic medications and the availability of staff who are skilled in non-pharmacological management of behavioural and psychological symptoms in dementia.

- Psychological therapy resources should be made available for people with dementia and their carers.
- Further research should be carried out, including studies of non-pharmacological methods of treating behavioural problems in dementia and of alternative pharmacological treatments. (Banerjee 2009)

Most of the concern about inappropriate drug use in people with dementia has focused on antipsychotic prescribing. But, of course, other drug groups are also used inappropriately at times. The use of hypnotics, or sleeping tablets, should generally be frowned upon, certainly other than for short periods in particular situations. Disturbance of the sleep–wake cycle is common in dementia, particularly in Lewy body dementia and also in Alzheimer's disease; it is part of the condition and using hypnotics won't change this. Often what happens when these drugs are used is that the person it is prescribed to still gets restless, may get up, is a bit groggy and unsteady, and may fall and sustain an injury. In addition, tolerance to these drugs develops over a few weeks and they lose their effect.

Diazepam and other related drugs and antidepressants such as trazodone may also be used to help manage behaviour. But use should be carefully thought through and should be only implemened as a last resort – that is, when non-pharmacological means have been used without success.

Previous chapters in this book have shown clearly how sleep disturbance and night-time challenging behaviour can be induced by the environment and staff practices, which can be changed. This helps prevent many of the behaviours that are presently treated with medication. Appropriately trained staff will also be better able to manage disturbed behaviours in a way that does not cause them to escalate. It is worth noting that Banerjee comments in his report that 'the proportion of these prescriptions which would be unnecessary if appropriate support were available is unclear and will vary by setting, but may well be of the order of two-thirds overall' (2009, p.6).

It is, of course, not the job of night staff to prescribe, but it is often the story and interpretation of a person and their behaviour that they give to the prescribing practitioner that will determine the drug given. It is important, therefore, that staff are aware of the need to be sensitive to explanations for night-time behaviours and to look at other ways to prevent and manage the problems. Much that has been written in this book should arm staff with alternative interpretations, understanding and responses to people in their care at night.

Drugs ought to be used only as a last resort. As suggested throughout this book, there are other, safer, ways to respond to agitation, 'wandering', sleeplessness, aggression and other forms of so-called 'challenging behaviour'.

The challenge for night staff is to identify triggers for 'challenging' behaviour and to either remove them or remove the person with dementia from the trigger.

Often the medication section of an assessment form is seen as something that the doctor or nurse completes and only to be used to state the types of medication the person is currently on. Information also needs to be recorded to inform carers and clinicians of the person's other needs relating to the taking of medication and this may include things that only the night staff are privy to.

## Methods of taking medication

People will have different responses to taking medication. Some people will be resistant to any form of medication. Some will have problems with taking tablets and others may be quite happy to take anything given. Some people may have a preference for taking medication in a liquid form; others may dislike taking tablets that dissolve.

People's responses will be determined by their previous experiences of taking medication, their beliefs about the need and advisability of taking medication and their ability to swallow.

People may also have preferences or routines that help them take medication – for example, the person may like to take tablets with a particular drink; another person may have a routine about how to use an inhaler. There may be an issue about night-time medication. People, especially people with dementia, may not be as able to take medication at night as they are during the day. They may be able to swallow and understand what they are being given and why during the day, but at night they may be suspicious of the medication and may have difficulty swallowing. It is important that night staff are clear about the differences between day and night-time responses and abilities.

The way in which a medication is given must at all times follow pharmaceutical manufacturers' legal and clinical guidelines. For example, certain tablet medications should not be crushed or taken with other medications (Wright *et al.* 2006). If a person has specific swallowing difficulties or receives medication through a tube, then clinical guidance on this should also be followed thoroughly. The use of liquid medication, medication that dissolves under the tongue and transdermal patch may all provide a useful range of options to help people receive the right treatment in the right dose with the least disruption.

As with many aspects of the care of people who have conditions that may mean that they are not able to make decisions for themselves, the administration of medication needs to consider the issue of capacity. Does the person have the capacity to determine whether he wants or needs to take the medication? Does he understand the consequences of not taking it? Does he understand the implications of taking it? Legislation* is in place to make sure that people who may not have full capacity are protected and given recognition of the capacity that they do retain. Night staff may well have information about a person at night that may influence the assessment of their capacity.

---

\*     www.publicguardian.gov.uk/mca/mca.htm for England and Wales and www.opsi.gov.uk/legislation/scotland/acts2000/asp_20000004_en_1 in Scotland.

# Summary

The development of various conditions of older age means that many older people will be taking more than one form of medication. If this is not closely monitored, there is a possibility of adverse reactions, either to a new drug or to the impact of the polypharmacy, where a number of different drugs are taken in combination.

The impact of polypharmacy can lead to the development of an acute confusional state or delirium. This may mimic the various characteristics of dementia and may lead night staff to wrongly think that someone's dementia is developing more quickly or that someone without dementia has suddenly developed the condition.

People with dementia are at risk of displaying challenging behaviour. It is important to remember that, whilst actions such as 'wandering', shouting, hitting out at others or generally being uncooperative often present a challenge to the providers of care, the person may be trying to communicate something which, if understood, may require a response other than medication. Where medication is used, it is essential that night staff administer it strictly to the guidelines.

# Acknowledgements

With thanks to Dr Graham Jackson for his comments on this chapter.

# Chapter 12

# End-of-Life and Palliative Care at Night

### CASE STUDY 30

Bill was in the final stages of life, and staff thought that he only had days left. His key worker had spent some time with his wife and son talking through his symptoms and needs and asking them what involvement they would like. Bill's son and wife were taking it in turns to sit with Bill. The care home staff put a comfortable reclining chair in Bill's room with some blankets for when one of them stayed with Bill through the night. The family was also supported by a visiting palliative care nurse who also supported the staff when they had questions or needed help with any of the healthcare procedures. Bill died with his wife and son with him early one morning. The night staff were there and were able to support Bill's wife and son as Bill died and in the hours thereafter.

For many staff and care home residents, part of the common experience of working or living in a care home is that of death and bereavement. A central part of the care provided within a care home is in supporting good end-of-life and palliative care.

End-of-life care is used to describe the support and interventions given to people who are approaching death. A key aspect of this is to make the person comfortable and to attend to their needs and wishes in the final stages of dying and as their death approaches. Palliative care usually covers a much longer period of care over the last months and weeks of someone's life. The World Health Organization describes palliative care as 'an approach that improves the quality of life of patients and their families facing the problem associated with life-threatening illness, through the prevention and relief of suffering by means of early identification and impeccable assessment and treatment of pain and other problems, physical, psychosocial and spiritual' (WHO 2002). Within the National Dementia Strategy for England and Wales (2009), developing good end-of-life care, including communication and planning around end of life, have all been identified as priorities.

More older people living in care homes are also dying there rather than in a hospital or a hospice (Katz 2004; Marie Curie Cancer Care 2009) and this trend is likely to continue. This makes it imperative that all care home staff, day and night staff, know about the issues around death and dying and that they are trained and supported to work with people who are dying, their relatives and other residents (Sidell 2003).

Ensuring that staff in care homes have appropriate palliative care training is identified as one of the most important means of improving the quality of care for someone when dying (Dalley and Denniss 2001; Froggatt and Hault 2002; Komaromy, Sidell and Katz 2000; Nolan, Featherston and Nolan 2003; Sidell 2003). As already noted in Chapter 2, night staff may have reduced access to appropriate training. One of the most difficult issues for care home staff is being able to talk about death and dying with residents and relatives. This, therefore, needs to be given priority in any training that is offered. Night staff have an essential role in end-of-life care as they will have a specific relationship and knowledge of the resident which is so useful in making sure that the resident's health and emotional needs are met. They will also have information that they can share with relatives about how their loved one has been through the night.

Supporting someone who is dying can be a heavy caring and emotional load, especially as care home staff may have known the resident for some time (Small, Froggatt and Downs 2007). Often night staff are part of a much smaller team which can have both positive and negative effects when dealing with emotions. A small tight team can be very supportive of each other, but it can also result in fewer people sharing the emotional and the caring load. In addition to dealing with their own emotions, staff need to be able to support each other, relatives and other residents with their feelings and grief, as well as meeting the care needs of the person at the end of their life. Despite the emotional and physical demands, staff often feel great satisfaction at being able to do this well, providing dignity and 'a good death'.

The intimacy of the night-time can mean that night staff find themselves much more involved with the dying person. The night staff member may be alone with the person as they die, with little other support around. During the day many other staff may be involved in the final stages and in supporting each other. Some staff think that night-time is a time when people can experience a 'better' death as there is a calm rarely experienced during the day. The home is peaceful, staff have more time and families can be well supported when they are with their relative.

## The dying process

The process of dying is unique to each person. Although *when* a person is going to die is fairly uncertain, towards the very end of life this becomes more predictable. What is important, however, is that both palliative care and end-of-life policies and procedures are understood and implemented by night staff. The dying process can be daunting and demanding of everyone involved at an emotional as well as a physical level, and this has to be acknowledged and attended to.

## Care pathways

In order to improve the ways in which end-of-life and palliative care is understood and provided in care homes, a number of 'care pathways' have been developed. Few of these mention night-time care and most of them are aimed at supporting people with cancer. Two key examples are:

- the Gold Standards Framework (www. goldstandardsframework.nhs.uk)
- the Liverpool Care Pathway (Ellershaw and Wilkinson 2005).

These are as relevant to night staff as to any other staff involved in the care of the dying person.

The Gold Standards Framework was originally developed for use in primary care. In 2004 it was adapted for use in care homes and includes an accredited training programme.

The Liverpool Care Pathway has been developed by the Royal Liverpool University Hospitals and the Marie Curie Centre to transfer the hospice model of care into other care settings. The focus of the pathway is on the care culture and creating a clear plan of how care will be provided during the dying process. The process of creating a plan allows for staff and relatives' involvement and negotiation, and it is important that night staff are included in this process. The Liverpool Care Pathway has three sections: initial assessment, ongoing assessment, and care after death. Each section focuses on improving quality of care. The Pathway is updated frequently and full details are available online at: www.mariecurie. org.uk/forhealthcareprofessionals/liverpoolcarepathway.htm or www.mcpcil.org.uk/liverpool-care-pathway/index.htm.

## Recognising the end of life

A crucial part of providing end-of-life care is for staff to be able to identify the signs of approaching end of life. In the process of recognising signs, communication between day and night staff becomes crucial. Some of the signs may be more noticeable either during the night or the day, and communication between shifts is important so that all staff are updated of changes.

For people with dementia, there are often some very clear signs that they have entered the later stages of dying. They will generally experience the following:

- forget how to eat and drink
- be unable to sit up
- lose the ability to maintain balance
- find walking increasingly difficult
- lose bowel and bladder control
- become significantly less active
- experience changes in their metabolism
- have substantial weight loss
- experience the loss of short- and long-term memories
- lose their ability to recognise most previously familiar people and environments
- experience seizure activity
- become bedridden
- be at greater risk of choking and becoming dehydrated
- be at great risk of infection
- develop aspiration pneumonia
- develop hypertonia
- experience complete loss of self-care.

Crucially, staff should be aware that the person will still experience or be aware of familiar sounds and smells, so it is important to provide sensual experiences, touch, smells and music. The person will need company and not to be left alone, so familiar staff, friends and relatives are very important. Often it will be night staff who will have the quiet time to spend with a person.

For people with conditions other than dementia, there may be many of the same signs but sometimes these are not so obvious until later on. Certainly when the person is bedridden and is not eating or drinking enough to sustain life, then the end is close and the person is on the dying pathway, and staff need to have very clear guidelines and ideas about what needs to be done.

A critical issue by this stage is the potential for the development of pressure sores. This is an issue as soon as the person becomes bedridden or is spending increasing amounts of time not moving voluntarily. The provision of special mattresses and regular turning are essential. Pressure sores are preventable and may indicate inadequate attention and poor care. Once the person is less mobile, advice must be sought from a pressure sore care specialist. The specialist will use a specific ratings chart to check the condition of the person's skin. Their advice must be followed diligently and without variation. Much of the advice will include the following:

- Change clothes regularly – sweaty clothes can cause irritation.
- If the person is confined to bed, turn them every two hours. Use a special mattress that reduces pressure areas (air mattress) for chairs, wheelchairs and beds.
- Keep bedding loose.
- Use recommended cream on pressure areas such as hips, sacrum, heels, shoulders and buttocks.
- Maintain activity levels as much as possible (active or passive movement).
- A good diet will help to keep the skin healthier and more resistant to sores.
- Pay constant attention to hydration. People should drink 1–1.5 litres of fluid a day. Without this, the skin dries and cracks easily.
- Use baby oil on skin after washing. If talcum powder is needed, use sparingly.

- Use non-perfumed washing powders and fabric conditioners.

- Ensure that incontinence is dealt with appropriately. This will require ongoing assessment of appropriate continence aids.

- Ensure that urine and faeces do not remain in contact with the skin.

- Avoid tight and uncomfortable clothing.

- Ensure that there are no rough seams in clothing.

- Check that no objects are left in pockets as these can cause friction.

- Ensure that people are thoroughly dried after bathing, particularly in the skin folds. Under breasts, the groin area and underarms need special attention. Pat rather than rub dry.

- Always seek reassessment and ongoing support from the community or palliative care nurse. Ask the specialist nurse for a monitoring chart and complete regularly.

- Handover needs to specifically include details of pressure sore care.

- The lack of activity will also often lead to an increased risk of infection, especially pneumonia.

(Dodd, Kerr and Fern 2006)

## A good death

The focus of care work at this stage is to ensure that the person has 'a good death'. This requires planning, preparation and good communication. The planning needs to include the provision of appropriate medication, agreement on interventions and clear understanding about levels and quality of family involvement. It is essential that staff have worked with the palliative care nurse and the GP to set up systems and provision that will enable the person's final days to be as good as possible. In particular, check that the appropriate medications (for the relief of agitation, pain and moist chest) have been prescribed and that staff are clear about when and how to use these. These drugs need to be monitored carefully.

The issue of pain relief at end-stage is critical. Much has been written in Chapter 10 on pain recognition and management. All this applies to the end of life with the added caveat that people may be less able to indicate pain and yet may well be experiencing an increase in their pain levels.

## Staffing issues

There are a number of issues to consider around staffing when a resident is dying. The most important is having flexible staffing hours available, particularly extra staff time available during the night to sit with the person. Good support for staff during this time is a crucial part of the management task. For many homes, most end-of-life care will be provided by staff with limited input from any specialist palliative care staff. The need and desire for more specialist palliative care involvement was highlighted by Froggatt 2004.

Although it is important that the dying person has someone with them through the night, in some homes there is no guarantee that the level of staffing will permit this. The authors have been told by night staff that the inability to give this level of attention to a dying person is distressing for them, and, of course, one can only imagine the possible distress to the dying person.

Night staff cover might need to be increased or the night-time tasks shared differently. Shorter shifts will also help staff manage the additional caring and emotional challenges of supporting someone at the end of their life.

There needs to be a set of clear and known protocols in place to help night staff know which actions to take and when. Staff need to have clear guidelines about when to contact the doctor, the manager and relatives. It is essential that it is clear who is responsible for taking actions: for example, is it the key worker, the senior night staff or someone else? Decisions about calling the doctor and informing relatives need to be made, and the person responsible for making such decisions needs to know she has that authority. Calling relatives will be and indeed should be determined by previous discussion with the family. There may be occasions if someone dies during the night shift when it is appropriate to wait until morning to inform relatives. Other relatives may want to be called immediately.

## CASE STUDY 31

Christina has been working as the senior night nurse in a care home for 14 years. Her experience is that when it comes to informing and involving relatives, nothing should be assumed. She has found that some relatives are very annoyed and have on occasions lodged a compliant if they have not been informed immediately of their relative's death, even if this was at 2 a.m. Other relatives have been pleased not to have been woken.

Christina says that it is essential to talk to relatives, if possible, before the death to establish what they want. Where no such agreement has been established, Christine says that she will often veer on the side of delay: 'The announcement of the death will throw the family into grief and distress, and they might as well have a good night's sleep before dealing with the emotional and physical consequences of the death.'

## Relatives

Involving relatives where appropriate is an important part of providing good end-of-life care. For relatives of someone who is reaching the end of life, communication is essential: 'effective communication between relatives and staff remains the central issue, and required even more attention at this difficult time' (Woods, Keady and Seddon 2007, p.98).

Night staff have important information to communicate. 'What kind of night did he have?' is often a question from relatives. Ensuring good communication with relatives can take up staff time, so the beginning or end of a night shift can be when this time is made available. Clear, timely and sensitive communication between decision-makers, including medical staff, care staff, residents and their families is essential.

Relatives may feel a range of emotions from grief and bereavement to anger and guilt. Often staff find it difficult to talk to relatives about the impending death of their loved one. Smith (1998) found, however, that relatives do not want the subject avoided and often welcome the opportunity to talk to staff about what is to come. Relatives place a very high value on the relationship with care home staff, especially having someone familiar and comforting during the last stages of care (Lloyd 2000). One of the most important, but also possibly one of the most difficult, issues to communicate is when treatment is no longer possible and that the option is then for a well-planned and well-implemented process of terminal care (Field and Froggatt 2003; Travis *et al.* 2002; Porock *et al.* 2005).

As highlighted by Woods *et al.* (2007), what relatives really want to see is that their relative is being cared for, and this centres on pain control, keeping the person clean and dry, and a good caring attitude shown by staff. From their work they recommend several key actions, several of which tie in with a care pathway approach:

- Use a terminal stage care conference so that staff duties and responsibilities are clear to all.
- Provide information about the care home procedures.
- Avoid using euphemisms about death.
- Have a clear care plan about the decisions and processes during the end-of-life stage.

- Offer accommodation to relatives so that they can stay with their loved one.
- Allow both staff and residents to mark the death.

Responsibilities of the home towards relatives include informing relatives sensitively, allowing relatives to visit the person's room and giving them time to clear the room, handing over possessions in a sensitive way, and offering support and signposts to other support.

## Summary

The provision of good end-of-life and palliative care is an essential part of the care provided within a care home. Night staff need to be as well equipped, trained and supported as day staff.

The dying process can be daunting and demanding of everyone involved at an emotional as well as a physical level, and this has to be acknowledged and attended to. The use of care pathways can help to create a clear plan, which involves staff, relatives and the dying person in decisions about end-of-life care. Planning should include the provision of appropriate medication, agreement on interventions and clear understanding about levels and quality of family involvement. Night staff must be equal partners in this process.

Staff often need extra support at these times. Staffing issues to consider include having flexible staffing hours available, particularly extra staff time available during the night to sit with the person. Night staff cover might need to be increased or the night-time tasks shared differently. Shorter shifts will also help staff manage the additional caring and emotional challenges of supporting people at the end of their life.

Staff also need to have a set of clear and known protocols about when to contact the GP, manager and relatives.

# Chapter 13

# Relatives and Night-Time Care

Most people who enter a care home will have been living with or been supported by one or more relatives. Often the point at which people enter a care home is when the caring family members or friends feels unable to continue, perhaps because of their own failing health or because of changes in the needs of the other person that make living at home no longer viable. For family carers, the admission of their relative to a care home can often be a traumatic and distressing event, even where they acknowledge the need for such a move.

Prior to admission, most relatives will have been giving 24-hour care. Even where the carers, as with sons and daughters, are not living 24 hours with their relative, they will have been on 24-hour alert and usually they will have had every day punctuated by the care needs of their parent. Suddenly such 24-hour involvement changes and the carer can be left with an empty space. Although this can lead to a sense of relief, it is more likely that the carer will be left also with a sense of guilt and depression. It is important that staff recognise the emotional, psychological and physical impact that the admission has on the relative.

The admission to care does not relieve the carer of their emotional and psychological involvement. Zarit and Whitlatch (1993) found that:

> The careers of caregivers do not stop at the institution's
> door, but continue in an altered and still stressful way.
> Caregivers do not give up their role, they shift their
> responsibility. (p.35)

This shift can be very hard for carers to negotiate. They can be torn between wanting to continue to give the care and support that they had previously given and wanting the staff to take over many difficult and painful aspects of caring. For many carers, the tension is revisited every time they visit the home. Watching staff perform tasks they used to do can be very deskilling and make them feel useless or even guilty that they are not doing the things that a 'stranger ' is doing for the person they love. What can easily develop is a feeling amongst relatives that they are not wanted, needed or indeed valued by the staff, and a feeling amongst staff that relatives are checking up on them, are critical and do not understand the pressures that the staff are under.

Relatives may find the feelings engendered so distressing that they are anxious about visiting. It is, of course, very important for residents that contact with their spouse, children and friends is maintained. It is the role of management and direct care staff to develop systems and interactions that make it possible and easy for relatives to remain involved and for all to work in partnership to maintain the contact and relationship where this is needed and wanted.

## Communication

To maintain maximum and easy contact, it is essential that an efficient and sensitive communication structure be set up. Poor communication with relatives means that often they have false notions about the rules that exist about visiting, helping and general involvement. Schwartz and Vogel (1990) found that lack of communication and understanding between staff and relatives led to an ambiguity about roles where family members' willingness to help out was not recognised or perhaps was even unwelcome.

In almost all care homes staff feel that they could do more if they had more help, and yet relatives, who are often very willing to contribute, feel unable or hesitant to do so. This problem, which no doubt exists throughout the day, is exacerbated at night. Kerr *et al.* (2008) found that some relatives were not sure if they would be allowed to be in the home at night. They had not checked this out and were, therefore, basing this on a feeling rather than a fact. Some relatives would want to be involved in hands-on caring. This would involve undressing and dressing the person for bed, supporting them to eat, helping them to the toilet and perhaps even giving medication.

Of course, this raises all sorts of issues about accountability, responsibility and health and safety. Staff may be concerned that relatives will sustain some sort of injury if they are involved in lifting and handling or that medication will not be administered properly. These are tricky areas and the correct protocols, policies and procedures need to be adhered to. It is important that these are communicated to and discussed with relatives. Communication is also vital if staff are going to have a full and meaningful understanding of the resident. If care is going to be person-centred, then a vital component is that staff know the person, her history, her likes and dislikes and her routines. If the person has dementia, then relatives are usually the key informants and so need to be encouraged and valued for the information that they can provide. The development of life story work as described in Chapter 9 is critical to this process.

In relation to night care, night staff need to know the person's night-time routines, likes and dislikes. Did the person like the light on, did he always read before he went to sleep, did he keep the radio on, did he do exercises, did he do the crossword, did he say prayers, did he wear pyjamas or sleep naked, did he always have a bath/shower before bed, and so on. Keeping to such routines can help the person settle at night, and for people with dementia, it can help orientation and give cues that indicate that it is bedtime.

One way to facilitate the gaining of such information is through a night-time key worker system. Care homes often have a daytime key worker system but rarely an appointed or named person for each resident at night. It is vital that information about the resident is passed to night staff, but also that night staff are clear about the type of information they need. This might be very different from the things that the daytime key worker focuses on.

## Involvement of relatives

Woods, Keady and Seddon (2007) found that many family members wanted continued involvement but were uncertain about what was possible and even what was allowed. It is essential that the home makes the encouragement of relatives' involvement explicit and takes the lead in this. This can be done through information giving, interaction between staff, management and relatives, and proactively seeking relatives who want to be involved and even take part in activities.

Realistically, most of these activities are going to be during the day. Few relatives do visit at night because of other commitments, health issues and general tiredness, as well as uncertainty about their role. However, it is important to make sure that such involvement that relatives do want to have at night is not being squandered or ignored. There is something of a paradox that at night, when staffing levels are low, relatives feel that they would be in the way. It could be immensely helpful to have relatives present to help, provided that they have clear guidelines about what is needed and what is acceptable.

It is also important to recognise that different people will have different abilities, needs and motivations, and that they may have ideas of their own about what activities and involvement they could offer.

## CASE STUDY 32

Sally Adam's mother had been in the care home for six weeks and staff reported that she was very restless at night. She would sit in bed with a book but would not read it and would become agitated and sometimes shout at staff. Sally knew that her mother had always been a keen reader and had always read before going to sleep. Sally started to go in at night to read to her mother. This proved to be an immense success and Sally's mother went to sleep contented.

Eventually the home manager asked if Sally would come in regularly and read to other residents. This was very successful, but only if Sally read to her mother first.

Clearly this would be impractical for most relatives, but homes might well benefit from making a clear invitation to relatives to undertake such work. Often relatives want to be able to contribute but do not know how. For relatives who are at work and unable to visit in the day, this could be an excellent way to enable them to be in the home at night.

## Lack of knowledge and anxiety about the night-time care

## CASE STUDY 33

Rose's mother has been living in the Elms Care Home for nine months. Her mother has dementia. Rose commented that she had never met a member of the night staff and often worried about what went on at night.

Her mother talks about people Rose does not know and she wonders if these are night staff or someone from her mother's past.

Rose comes into the home every other day and so knows the day staff well. She hopes the night staff are 'as nice' and that they know her mother as well 'because she can be difficult and I worry they might not be patient with her'.

Like many relatives of people in care homes, Rose knew nothing about night-time routines or night staff. Kerr *et al.* (2008) found that relatives, even if they spent time in the home during the day, had very little information about night-time care. They felt that they were 'in the dark' about night-times. Relatives rarely met night staff and were anxious about who they were and what they were like. The following quotation is pertinent:

> But I knew nothing about night. But I kind of found out by default what was going on because a member of the night staff was doing an extra shift in the laundry during the day. And as we were going past, I didn't know she was obviously a night staff. But she said 'oh hi' to my mum. And said to me 'oh your mum's a character, you know'. And she then started chatting. It was very reassuring, hugely reassuring. It was just nice to know that there's nice people on at night. (Kerr *et al.* 2008, p.28)

Considerable anxiety can be felt by relatives about what happens at night (Kerr *et al.* 2008). Their concerns were expressed in very similar ways to those expressed by night staff themselves and they often asked the question 'what if?':

> What if there was a fire or another emergency, there are not enough staff to get everyone out.

> Unless they are super heroes they will never get them out in a fire, there's no way two people are coping with all these people and a fire.

The fact that no one had actually asked about the procedure was, perhaps, indicative of a fear about what they would be told:

> And that's, that's my worry and again I think maybe that's why we don't ask because we don't want to know really.

The reality is that the small number of staff who work at night may not be able to evacuate all the residents if there was a major fire. This is a terrifying prospect for any relative who begins to think about this issue. It might be helpful for relatives to be shown the fire procedures policy.

This finding was replicated in a study carried out in Ireland (Woods *et al.* 2007) where relatives reported feeling anxious and 'out of control' regarding care at night and early morning. They were also aware of the low staffing levels at night and 'could not see how the staff could possibly cope' (p.47).

Members of one relatives' group who took part in the Kerr *et al.* (2008) research suggested that having photographs of night staff on display would help give them a sense of who the staff were, what they looked like and what they were called. This might also help with conversations with the resident. Often care homes do have staff photographs up, but often they only feature day staff.

An additional concern raised by residents queried night-time inspection procedures (Kerr *et al.* 2008) and came from recognition by relatives that night-times do not necessarily bring calm and sleep to their relative but that:

> The problems that residents have in the day won't go away at night-time.

Their worry that there would be problems dealing with an emergency meant that relatives wanted tighter controls and inspections at night. Such inspections may not directly lead to any safer night-time emergency practice, but a lack of inspection underlined the sense that at night their relatives were not being given the same level of attention and value as they were during the day.

## Relatives' involvement in end-of-life care

Night staff often says that the time that they get to know relatives is when the resident is close to death. Relatives will often spend nights in the home. They need to have much support and privacy. They also need to have space for themselves to sleep and rest. Woods *et al.* (2007) comment that 'relatives should be offered accommodation to stay in the home during the final stages if they wish' (p.114).

Day staff will be involved with relatives at the end of life of residents, but night staff have a particular role to play. People are more likely to die at night, and relatives are more isolated from their own supports at night and will be more likely to seek support from night staff. Staff need support and training to cope, including training to provide palliative care and to counsel bereaved and grieving relatives (Woods *et al.* 2007). Night staff often don't have access to the same training opportunities as day staff. It is, however, essential that their involvement with relatives at such difficult and painful times is recognised and that they are properly equipped to deal with situations that arise. This is more important because night staff often feel isolated and vulnerable themselves (Kerr *et al.* 2008).

## Summary

Usually before moving into a care home, most people will have been living with or been supported by one or more relatives. For these relatives, the admission of their loved one to a care home can often be a traumatic and distressing event, even where they acknowledge the need for such a move. They can be left with an empty space after providing high levels of care. It is important that staff recognise the emotional, psychological and physical impact that the admission has on the relatives.

Relatives need to know that it's OK to visit at night and to be involved in hands-on caring if they wish. Night staff need to find out from relatives about the night-time routines, likes and dislikes of the resident if the resident is unable to communicate this for herself. The presence of a relative at night can be calming and reassuring for the resident and this should be supported where the relative feels able to be present. Issues of accountability, responsibility and health and safety must be clear.

# Chapter 14

# Night-Time
# Care Prompts
# for Inspectors

Across the UK there are national bodies with responsibility for monitoring and regulating a series of care standards. These are:

- England – Care Quality Commission (CQC)
- Wales – Care and Social Services Inspectorate for Wales (CSSIW)
- Scotland – Scottish Commission for the Regulation of Care
- Northern Ireland – Northern Ireland Social Care Council (NISCC)

Within each national body, officers (inspectors and regulators) play a vital role in ensuring that care services are of an acceptable quality according to established standards and guidance (for more information visit the Office of Public Sector Information website at www.opsi.gov.uk and see the 'Further reading' section at the end of this chapter).

The standards describe the overarching principles that must inform the service provided in a care home, but they do not make any specific reference to the needs of older people at night.

For a variety of logistical and financial reasons, care homes are not inspected with the same level of rigour at night as they are during the day. As evidenced throughout this book, the night-time is not a dormant time but a period of activity both amongst staff and residents. Therefore, it is important that this activity is as open to scrutiny as daytime activity. Night-time care should be understood, monitored and evaluated.

It should not be assumed that one could extrapolate from what goes on in the day to what goes on at night. Different staff, different activities and different needs require specific attention from managers and inspectors.

Following the findings from a research study *Supporting Older People in Care Homes at Night* (Kerr *et al.* 2008), staff from the University of Edinburgh and members of three of the inspection and regulatory bodies for the UK set up a short-term working group.* The remit of this group was to develop some guidance that would help inspectors of care homes to develop a clearer picture and understanding of night-time requirements in relation to activities, interactions, staffing levels and skills and environment.

A guidance tool was produced by the Commission for Social Care Inspection (CSCI) and now is available through the CQC website (www.cqc.org.uk).

Below we have reproduced the guidelines, with a few minor changes and omissions.

---

## NIGHT-TIME CARE PROMPTS
## GUIDANCE FOR INSPECTORS OF CARE HOMES

### What are night-time care prompts?

- The prompts are questions about how care homes make sure they provide effective night-time care.

---

* The work of this group was funded by the Joseph Rowntree Foundation between 2008–2010.

- The prompts help you think about how a service makes sure that night-time care and support are given as much recognition and attention as daytime care.
- They are based on the recommendations of a Joseph Rowntree Trust report.

The full report is available at www.cqc.org.uk/_db/_documents/20090220_Night_care_prompts_021-09.doc

## When should I use these prompts?

- At all stages of regulatory activity: planning fieldwork, writing hypotheses, during fieldwork, analysing evidence, writing reports, registering a service and during management reviews.

## How should I use them?

- These prompts help you to evaluate how well a service is meeting people's night-time care needs. They are based upon similar principles to daytime care needs.
- The list is not exhaustive and should not be used as a checklist or a set of direct questions to ask.
- They are not intended to replace observation of the environment or staff relationships with people living in the home.
- The prompts can be used flexibly and in the way that helps you best at different times in your regulatory activity.

## How do they relate to the KLORA?

- KLORA help us to make judgements about a service and should be used alongside these prompts.

KLORA stands for Key Lines of Regulatory Assessment – this is the guidance that inspectors use to help them assess evidence for social care services.

# Choice of home
## Key outcomes

People are confident that the care home can support them. This is because there is an accurate assessment of their needs that they, or people close to them, have been involved in. This tells the home all about them, what they hope for and want to achieve, and the support they need.

## Night-time care outcomes

People feel that their night-time care needs will be met because there are sufficient night staff who have the right knowledge and skills to plan and deliver the care they need.

## Questions to consider...

- Are people's night-time care needs identified with them and/or their representative before they move into the home?
- Does the needs assessment include:
  - continence
  - pain management
  - nutrition and hydration
  - medication
  - dementia care
  - their preference for male or female carers?
- Does the home have sufficient and suitable night staff to meet these needs?

# Individual needs and choices
## Key outcomes

People's needs and goals are met. The home has a plan of care that the person, or someone close to them, has been involved in making. People are able to make decisions about their life, including their finances, with support if they need it. This is because staff promote their rights and choices.

People have support to take risks to enable them to stay independent. This is because the staff have appropriate information on which to base decisions.

## Night-time care outcomes

People are asked about their choices for night-time care and those choices are respected.

## Questions to consider...

- Are people able to make choices about:
  - when they go to bed and when they get up in the morning
  - their routines when going to bed and getting up
  - their bed and bedding (for example, height of bed, number of pillows, type of mattress)
  - their personal care and the level of support they want at night
  - their preference for male or female carers?
- Are these choices included in their care plans along with any necessary risk assessments?
  - Are risk assessments completed and agreed with the individual, and/or their representatives?

# Daily life and social activities
## Key outcomes

Each person is treated as an individual and the care home is responsive to his or her race, culture, religion, age, disability, gender, including gender identity, and sexual orientation. They can take part in activities that are appropriate to their age and culture and are part of their local community. The care home supports people to follow personal interests and activities.

People are able to keep in touch with family, friends and representatives and the home supports them to have appropriate personal, family and sexual relationships. People are as independent as they can be, lead their chosen lifestyle and have the opportunity to make the most of their abilities. Their dignity and rights are respected in their daily life. People have healthy, well-presented meals and snacks, at a time and place to suit them.

## Night-time care outcomes

People have enough stimulation and exercise through the day to help them sleep at night. Their nutritional and hydration needs are met during the night.

## Questions to consider...

- Does the home provide sufficient exercise and stimulation for people through the day so they are ready to sleep when they go to bed?
- Are people's night-time nutritional and hydration wishes and needs recorded and met during the night?

# Personal and healthcare support/ health and personal care
## Key outcomes

People receive personal support from staff in the way they prefer and want. Their physical and emotional health needs are met because the home has procedures in place that staff follow.

If people take medicine, they manage it themselves if they can. If they cannot manage their medicine, the care home supports them with it in a safe way.

## Night-time care outcomes

People's assessed night-time needs and wishes are recorded and shared with night staff.

## Questions to consider...

- Do care plans have a night-time section which addresses:
  - continence
  - pain management
  - nutrition and hydration
  - medication
  - dementia care
  - environmental issues
  - end-of-life care
  - night-time routines, sleep patterns, individual choices about rising and retiring times, preference for male or female carers, whether they wish to be checked during the night (dependent upon risk assessment)?
- Does the home have arrangements to ensure that information about individuals' night care is communicated between staff and to relatives as necessary. For example, by each person having a named and known night-time worker who links to a daytime key worker or key worker group?
- Are these named workers trained and responsible for carrying out risk assessments for night-time activities?
- Are the named workers supported in communicating with the resident, relatives and daytime staff as necessary. For example, given the time and skills?
- Are night staff who administer medication trained and deemed competent?

# Environment

## Key outcomes

People stay in a safe and well-maintained home that is homely, clean, comfortable, pleasant and hygienic.

## Night-time care outcomes

The environment helps people to have a good night's rest.

## Questions to consider…

- Is maintenance work undertaken when necessary to reduce noisy plumbing and floorboards, creaking or banging doors and so on?
- Are call systems loud or is there a pager system in use at night to reduce noise?
- Are dim lights used in communal areas before bedtime?
- Do bedrooms have dim lights or night lights to reduce sleep disturbance, create a calm environment and signal to people that it is night-time? If not, have night staff got torches so they don't have to switch on bright lights?
- Are light switches within easy reach if people want to get up independently during the night?
- Is the building warm enough and safe enough if people get up during the night?
- Is signage clear enough to help orientate residents if they leave their rooms during the night?

# Staffing
## Key outcomes

People have safe and appropriate support as there are enough competent, qualified staff on duty at all times. They have confidence in the staff at the home because checks have been done to make sure that they are suitable.

People's needs are met and they are supported because staff get the right training, supervision and support they need from their managers.

## Night-time care outcomes

People are supported at night-time by a staff team who are trained and experienced to meet their needs.

## Questions to consider...

- Are there sufficient staff to meet assessed night-time needs as recorded in care plans?
- Does the team have a suitable skill mix?
- Do managers actively engage in meeting the support needs of night staff, particularly with regard to training and supervision?
- Are night-time staff made aware of the importance of helping residents to have a good night's sleep by:
  - opening and shutting doors quietly
  - talking quietly in corridors or near bedrooms
  - avoiding unnecessary trips up and down corridors
  - only checking or waking people if necessary and as described in their care plan
  - keeping lights low?
- Do night staff have the right training to help them to meet people's needs? Do they have the same access to, amount, frequency and level of training as day staff?
- Is the training provided at suitable times?
- Is the content of training relevant to night-time care? Does it include:
  - understanding of the needs of people with dementia
  - pain management
  - nutrition and hydration
  - continence
  - medication administration (where appropriate)
  - environmental issues

- end-of-life care?
- Are sufficient, regular staff employed to work at night to minimise the use of agency and bank staff and ensure consistency of care?
- Do night-time staff communicate clearly and effectively with residents in a language they understand?
- Do staff have enough time and understanding to provide the comfort and company people need during the night?

## Conduct and management of the home/ Management and administration

### Key outcomes

People have confidence in the care home because it is run and managed appropriately.

People's opinions are central to how the home develops and reviews their practice, as the home has appropriate ways of making sure they continue to get things right.

The environment is safe for people and staff because health and safety practices are carried out.

### Night-time care outcomes

People are confident their night-time needs will be met in a well-managed safe service.

### Questions to consider...

- Is there an operational night care policy which includes clearly defined management and care roles and responsibilities?
- Does the registered manager or competent individual with designated responsibility regularly spend some time in the home after 11.00 p.m. to observe care practice?

- Is supervision of night staff undertaken by the registered manager or clearly delegated individuals who have a management role?
- Does the registered manager have a clear strategy for checking recommended night staff practices are in place?
- Do policies and procedures specifically identify and address night-time care issues such as:
  - risk
  - checking
  - dementia care
  - pain management
  - nutrition and hydration
  - continence
  - end-of-life care
  - medication
  - staff handovers
  - environmental and noise levels?
- Are handovers between night and day staff programmed in to allow time for clear communication between them?
- Are there other opportunities (for example, staff meetings) for night and day staff to share information and discuss practice?
- Are arrangements made so night key workers can communicate with relatives where appropriate?
- Are strategies in place to keep relatives informed about night-time care?

*Source:* Care Quality Commission 2009. Reprinted by permission of David Bawden.

This tool was produced to inform and help inspectors of care homes. It is noteworthy, however, that many managers of care homes have commented that they have found this a helpful guide for themselves and their staff when thinking about the provision of good night-time practice.

The guidelines, to a considerable extent, incorporate much that has been written about throughout this book.

## Summary

Throughout the UK there are bodies appointed to inspect, monitor and regulate the care provided within care homes. For a variety of logistical and financial reasons, night-time care within care homes is not inspected and monitored with the same level of rigour as daytime care. Following findings from a research study on night-time care (Kerr *et al.* 2008), one of the UK Commissions, charged with the monitoring and inspection of care homes, produced guidelines for inspectors to help them better monitor and inspect night-time care, even if it is not possible for night-time visits to be made. These guidelines, produced in this chapter, have also proved to be very helpful to managers of care homes.

## Further reading

For more information on care home standards in England, Scotland and Wales please refer to the following:

Care Standards Act 2000 (England) at www.legislation.gov.uk/ukpga/2000/14/contents.

Health and Social Care (Community Health and Standards) Act 2003 (England and Scotland) at www.legislation.gov.uk/ukpga/2003/43/introduction?view=extent.

The Care Homes (Amendment) (Wales) Regulations 2003 at www.opsi.gov.uk/legislation/wales/wsi2003/20030947e.htm.

Regulation of care (Scotland) Act 2000 at www.opsi.gov.uk/legislation/scotland/acts2001/en/01en08-a.htm.

## Chapter 15

# Conclusion

Night-time care has been an invisible part of research and specific policy guidelines, yet it is a substantial and critical part of 24-hour care in any care home. This book has sought to redress the balance by highlighting issues that are important to residents, night-time care staff, relatives, managers and inspectors of care home services.

The night-time is a time when residents hope to have peaceful uninterrupted sleep. The role of night staff is seen as primarily to promote such sleep. The reality is, however, that for many residents the night-time is not a period of peace. There are many reasons for the disruption to residents' sleep. Some of these are the consequence of certain aspects of ageing and, in particular, of dementia. Some are the consequence of staff behaviours and interactions, and some are the consequence of aspects of the physical environment.

This book has looked at ways in which these causes can be either removed or ameliorated. There has also been recognition that waking at night is not necessarily a bad thing and that staff need to be aware of ways in which wakeful periods can be made stress-free and even have positive outcomes.

The need for staff to have a good understanding of the needs of people with dementia, the management of night incontinence and how to meet nutritional needs, the recognition and management of pain and the provision of suitable activities have all been addressed. There is recognition of the fact that care through the night can be an opportunity to give emotional, physical, social and psychological support to people when they are often at their most vulnerable.

There has also been attention given to the physical environment and, in particular, aspects of the environment that need to be addressed to support people with dementia.

Night-time care cannot be viewed without attention to the needs of the carers. The quality of care and support given is inextricably linked to the health, skills, knowledge and attitudes of the staff. The experiences of night staff and the way in which these affect their abilities to care and manage the night-time care have been explored. Attention has also been given to the health implications for staff working either solely or regularly at night. There are serious health and social implications for people who work constantly on nights, and possible ways of alleviating the negative health and social aspects have been explored.

There is a clear role for management in developing a proactive engagement with night staff. Management involvement in the hours in the middle of the night enable a more rounded and accurate picture of the night-time world of the home. Management involvement and supervision of staff also helps to reduce the sense of isolation and anxiety often experienced by night staff.

The book highlights the need for the inspection of homes to be as rigorous during the night as it is during the day. Inspecting at night only when there is a complaint or cause for concern does not take account of the nature of the night-time environment or of the need to be certain that standards are maintained throughout the 24-hour period of care.

Finally, a plea for the future. Although there are undoubtedly homes where night-time care is well staffed, well managed and well inspected, this is not guaranteed and to an extent it is something of a lottery as to whether such well-resourced and managed night care exists. There is a need for night-times to be subjected to more scrutiny and research and to more specific policy guidelines.

That policy makers, service providers and managers of care homes are often not as alert to the demands, needs and reality of the night-time in a care home means that all the advances in the care of older people in care homes are not guaranteed to be integrated into night as they are through the care day. This is cause for concern and needs to be addressed seriously and urgently.

# References

Aarsland, D., Perry, R., Larsen, J.P., McKeith, I.G., O'Brien, J.T., Perry, E.K., Burn, D. and Ballard, C.G. (2005) 'Neuroleptic sensitivity in Parkinson's disease and parkinsonian dementias.' *Journal of Clinical Psychiatry 66*, 633–7.

Abbey, J.A., Pillier, N., DeBellis, A., Esterman, A., *et al.* (2004) 'The Abbey pain scale: A 1-minute numerical indicator for people with late-stage dementia.' *International Journal of Palliative Nursing 10*, 1, 6–13.

Alzheimer's Research Trust (2010) *Dementia 2010*. Oxford: Oxford University.

Amicus (2003) 'Amicus Guide to the Working Time Regulations.' Available at www.amicustheunion.org/pdf/workingtimeregsbrief.pdf, accessed on 13 May 2010.

Ancoli-Israel, S. and Aayalon, L. (2006) 'Diagnosis and treatment of sleep disorders in older adults.' *American Journal of Geriatric Psychiatry 14*, 95–103.

Ancoli-Israel, S., Parker, L. and Sinaee, R. (1997) 'Variations in circadian rhythms of activity, sleep and light exposure related to dementia in nursing home patients.' *Sleep 20*, 18–23.

Archibald, C. (2003) *People with Dementia in Acute Hospital Settings: A Practice Guide for Nurses*. Stirling: Dementia Services Development Centre.

Arendt, J. and Deacon, S. (1997) 'Treatment of circadian rhythm disorders – melatonin.' *Chronobiology International 14*, 185–204.

Armstrong-Esther, C.A., Browne, K.D., Armstrong-Esther, D.C. and Sander, L. (1996) 'The institutionalized elderly: Dry to the bone!' *International Journal of Nursing Studies 33*, 6, 619–28.

Asplund, R. and Aberg, H. (1991) 'Diurnal variation in the levels of antidiuretic hormone in the elderly.' *Journal of Internal Medicine 229*, 131–4.

Avidan A. (2006) 'Sleep and neurological problems in the elderly.' *Sleep Medicine Clinics 1*, 2, 273–92.

Avidan, A.Y., Fries, B.E., James, M.L., Szafara, K.L., Wright, G.T. and Chervin, R.D. (2005) 'Insomnia and hypnotic use, recorded in the minimum data set, as predictors of falls and hip fractures in Michigan nursing homes.' *Journal of American Geriatrics Society 53*, 6, 955–962.

Axelsson, G., Rylander, R. and Molin, I. (1989) 'Outcome of pregnancy in relation to irregular and inconvenient work schedules.' *British Journal of Industrial Medicine 46*, 393–8.

Banerjee, S. (2009) 'The use of antipsychotic medication for people with dementia: Time for action. A report for the minister of state for care services.' London: Department of Health.

Barber, R., Pannikar, A. and McKeith, I.G. (2001) 'Dementia with Lewy bodies: Diagnosis and management.' *International Journal of Geriatric Psychiatry 16* (Suppl. 1), S12–15.

Baxter, V. and Kroll-Smith, S. (2005) 'Normalizing the workplace nap: Blurring the boundaries between public and private space and time.' *Current Sociology 53*, 1, 33–55.

Bell, V., Troxel, D., Cox, T. and Hamon, R. (2004) *The Best Friends Book of Alzheimer's Activities Volume 1*. Baltimore, MD: Health Professionals Press.

Berger, A.M. and Hobbs, B.B. (2006) 'Impact of shift work on the health and safety of nurses and patients.' *Clinical Journal of Oncology Nursing 10*, 4.

Bisanti, L., Olsen, J. and Basso, O. (1996) 'Shift work and subfecundity: A European multicenter study.' *Journal of Occupational and Environmental Medicine 38*, 352–8.

Bloom, H.G., Ahmed, I., Alessi, C.A., Ancoli-Israel, S., *et al.* (2009) 'Evidence-based recommendations for the assessment and management of sleep disorders in older persons.' *Journal of the American Geriatrics Society 57*, 761–89.

Bonnefond, A., Muzet, A., Winter-Dill, A.S., Bailloeuil, C., Bitouze, F. and Bonneau, A. (2001) 'Technical note. Innovative working schedule: Introducing one short nap during the night shift.' *Ergonomics 44*, 10, 937–45.

Bootzin, R.R. and Perlis, M.L. (1992) 'Nonpharmacologic treatments of insomnia.' *Journal of Clinical Psychiatry 53*, 6 (Suppl.) 37–41.

Brawley, E.C. (1997) *Designing for Alzheimer's Disease.* New York: John Wiley & Sons.

Buijssen, H. (2005) *The Simplicity of Dementia: A Guide for Family and Carers.* London: Jessica Kingsley Publishers.

Bupa (2007) Personal Communication from Tim Brooke, Bupa Care Services.

Bupa (2009) 'Night bite menu.' Leeds: Bupa Care.

Burgess, N., Maguire, E.A. and O'Keefe, J. (2002) 'The human hippocampus and spatial and episodic memory.' *Neuron 35*, 625–41.

Burns, A., Howard, R. and Pettit, W. (1997) *Alzheimer's Disease: A Medical Companion.* Oxford: Blackwell Science.

Calkins, M.P. (1988) *Design for Dementia: Planning Environments for the Elderly and the Confused.* Owings Mills, MD: National Health Publishing.

Cantley, C. and Wilson, R.C. (2003) *Put Yourself in My Place: Designing and Managing Care Homes for People with Dementia.* Bristol: Policy Press.

Care Quality Commission (2009) *Night Time Care Prompts.* London: CQC. Available at www.cqc.org.uk/_db/_documents/20090408_Night_care_prompts_021-09_doc_rebranded.doc, accessed on 20 August 2010.

Cheston, R. and Bender, M. (1999) *Understanding Dementia: The Man with the Worried Eyes.* London: Jessica Kingsley Publishers.

Clancy, J. (2000) *Ordinary Time.* Ceredigion: Gomer.

Cohen, U. and Day, K. (1993) *Contemporary Environments for People with Dementia.* Baltimore, MD: John Hopkins University Press.

Cohen, U. and Weisman, G.D. (1991) *Holding on to Home: Designing Environments for People with Dementia.* Baltimore, MD: John Hopkins University Press.

Cohen-Mansfield, J., Werner, P. and Marx, M. (1990) 'Screaming in nursing home residents.' *Journal of American Geriatrics Society 38*, 785–92.

Costa, G. and Pokorski, J. (2000) 'Effects of Health and Medical Surveillance of Shift Workers.' In T. Marek, H. Oginska, J. Pokorski, G. Costa, S. Folkard (eds) *Shift Work 2000: Implications for Science, Practice and Business.* Krakow: Institute of Management, Jagiellonien University.

Dalley, G. and Denniss, M. (2001) *Trained to Care: Investigating the Skills and Competencies of Care Assistants in Homes for Older People.* London: Centre for Policy on Ageing.

Davis, S. and Mirick, D. (2006) 'Circadian disruption, shift work and the risk of cancer: A summary of the evidence and studies in Seattle.' *Cancer Causes Control 17*, 539–45.

Dawson, P. (1998) 'Cognitively impaired residents receive less pain medication than non-cognitively impaired residents.' *Perspectives 22*, 4, 16–17.

Del Ser, T., McKeith, I., Anand, R., Cicin-Sain, A., Ferrara, R. and Spiegel, R. (2000) 'Dementia with Lewy bodies: Findings from an international multicentre study.' *International Journal of Geriatric Psychiatry 15*, 11, 1034–45.

Department of Health (2009) *Living Well with Dementia: A National Dementia Strategy.* London: Department of Health.

Dinges, D.F., Orne, M.T., Whitehouse, W.G. and Orne, E.C. (1987) 'Temporal placement of a nap for alertness: Contributions of circadian phase and prior wakefulness.' *Sleep 10*, 4, 313–29.

Dingley, J. (1996) 'A computer-aided comparative study of progressive alertness changes in nurses working two different night-shift rotas.' *Journal of Advanced Nursing 23*, 6, 1247–53.

Djik, D.J., Duffy, J.F. and Reil, E. (1999) 'Ageing and the circadian and homeostatic regulation of human sleep during forced desynchrony of rest, melatonin and temperature rhythms.' *Journal of Physiology 516*, 2, 611–27.

Djik, D.J., Duffy, J.F. and Zeisler, C.A. (2001) 'Age-related increase in awakenings: Impaired consolidation of nonREM sleep at all circadian phases.' *Sleep 24*, 565–77.

Dodd, K., Kerr, D. and Fern, S. (2006) *Down's Syndrome and Dementia: A Workbook for Staff.* Teddington: Down's Syndrome Association.

Dugan, E., Roberts, C., Cohen, S., Preisser, J., Davis, C., Bland, D. and Albertson, E. (2001) 'Why older community-dwelling adults do not discuss urinary incontinence with their primary care physicians.' *Journal of American Geriatrics Society 49*, 4, 462–5.

Elia, M. (ed.) (2003) 'The "MUST" report. Nutritional screening for adults: A multidisciplinary responsibility. Development and use of the "Malnutrition Universal Screening Tool" ("MUST") for adults.' A report by the Malnutrition Advisory Group of the British Association for Parenteral and Enteral Nutrition, 2003, p.127. (See www.bapen.org.uk to download charts, tables and the procedures.)

Ellershaw and Wilkinson (2005) *The Liverpool Care Pathway for the Dying Patient.* Available at www.mcpcil. org.uk/liverpool-care-pathway, accessed on 13 May 2010.

Fader, M., Clarke-O'Neill, S. and Cook, D. (2003) 'Management of night-time urinary incontinence in residential settings for older people: An investigation into the effects of different pad changing regimes on skin health.' *Journal of Clinical Nursing 12*, 374–86.

Field D. and Froggatt K. (2003) 'Issues for Palliative Care in Nursing and Residential Homes.' In J.S. Katz and S.M. Peace (eds) *End of Life in Care Homes: A Palliative Care Approach.* Oxford: Oxford University Press.

Fiorentino, L. and Ancoli-Israel, S. (2006) 'Sleep disturbances in nursing home patients.' *Sleep Medicine Clinics 1*, 293–8.

Fitten, I.J., Morely, J.E., Gross, P.L., Petry, S.D. and Cole, K.D. (1989) 'Depression.' *Journal of American Geriatric Society 37*, 459-72.

Foley, D.J., Monjan, A.A. and Brown, S.L. (1995) 'Sleep complaints among older persons: An epidemiological study of three communities.' *Sleep 18*, 425–32.

Foley, D.J., Monjan, A.A. and Simonsick, E.M. (1999) 'Incidence and remission of insomnia among elderly adults: An epidemiological study of 6,800 persons over three years.' *Sleep 22* (Suppl.), S366–72.

Ford, G. (1996) 'Putting feeding back into the hands of the patients.' *Journal of Psychosocial Nursing and Mental Health Services 34*, 5, 35–9.

Froggatt, K. (2004) *Palliative Care in Care Homes for Older People.* London: The National Council for Palliative Care.

Froggatt, K.A. and Hoult, L. (2002) 'Developing palliative care practice in nursing and residential care homes: The role of the clinical nurse specialist.' *Journal of Clinical Nursing 11*, 6, 802–808

Garbarino, S., Mascialino, B., Penco, M.A., Squarcia, S., *et al.* (2004) 'Professional shift-work drivers who adopt prophylactic naps can reduce the risk of car accidents during night work.' *Sleep 27*, 2, 1295–1302.

Goldsmith, M. (1996) *Hearing the Voice of People with Dementia: Opportunities and Obstacles.* London: Jessica Kingsley Publishers.

Haan, M.N., Selby, J.V., Quesenberry, C.P., Schmittdiel, J.A., Fireman, B.H. and Rice, D.P. (1997) 'The impact of aging and chronic disease on use of hospital and outpatient services in a large HMO: 1971–1991.' *Journal of the American Geriatrics Society 45*, 667–74.

Hall, G.R. (1994) 'Chronic dementia: Challenges in feeding the patient.' *Journal of Gerontological Nursing 15*, 16–20.

Hansen, J. (2006) 'Risk of breast cancer after night and shift work: Current evidence and ongoing studies in Denmark.' *Cancer Causes and Control 17*, 4, 531–7.

Herr, K., Bjoro, K. and Decker, S. (2006) 'Tools for assessment of pain in nonverbal older adults with dementia: A state-of-the-science review.' *Journal of Pain and Symptom Management 31*, 2, 170–92.

Hiatt, L.G. (1995) 'Understanding the physical environment.' *Pride Institute Journal of Long Term Care 4*, 2, 12–22.

Holmes, J.A., Teresi, M., Ramirez, J., Ellis, J., Eimicke, J., Kong, L., Orzechowska, L. and Silver, S. (2007) 'An evaluation of a monitoring system intervention: Falls, injuries, and affect in nursing homes.' *Clinical Nursing Research 16*, 317–35.

Hopker, S. (1999) *Drug Treatments and Dementia (Bradford Dementia Group Good Practice Guide).* London: Jessica Kingsley Publishers.

Horgas, A. and Tsai, P. (1998) 'Analgesic drug prescription and use in cognitively impaired nursing home residents.' *Nursing Research 47,* 4, 235.

Horgas, A. and Elliot, A. (2001) 'Pain assessment and management in persons with dementia.' *Nursing Clinics of North America 39,* 3, 593–606.

Horgas, A.L., Nichols, A.L., Schapson, C.A. and Vietes, K. (2007) 'Assessing pain in persons with dementia: Relationships among the non-communicative patients pain assessment instrument, self-report and behavioural observations.' *Pain Management Nursing 8,* 2, 77–85.

Hornberger, S., Knauth, P., Costa, G. and Folkard, S. (eds) (2000) *Shift Work in the 21st Century.* Frankfurt: Peter Lang.

International Agency for Research on Cancer (2007) Press release No. 180, 5 December 2007.

International Labour Organisation (1990) 'C171 Night Work Convention.' Available at www.ilo.org/ilolex/cgi-lex/convde.pl?C171, accessed on 13 May 2010.

Iskra-Golec, I., Marek, T., Fafrowicz, M., Zieba, A. and Honory, B. (2000) 'The Effects of Bright Light on Performance and Mood in Morning and Evening People.' In S. Hornberger, P. Knauth, G. Costa, S. Folkard (eds) *Shift Work in the 21st Century.* Frankfurt: Peter Lang.

Jacques, A. and Jackson, G. (2000) *Understanding Dementia – Third Edition.* Edinburgh: Churchill Livingstone.

Jenkins, D.A.L. (1998) *Bathing People with Dementia: The Bathroom and Beyond.* Stirling: Dementia Services Development Centre.

Jones, K., Fink, R., Pepper, G., Hutt, E., *et al.* (2004) Improving nursing home staff knowledge and attitudes about pain.' *The Gerontologist 44,* 4, 469–78.

Jorm, A.F. and Jolley, D. (1998) 'The incidence of dementia: A meta-analysis.' *Neurology 51,* 728–33.

Judd, S., Marshall, M. and Phippen, P. (1998) *Design for Dementia.* London: Hawker Publications Limited.

Kahnoski, B. (2000) 'Shift work presents challenges to circadian rhythms.' *The Oregon Nurse 65,* 4, 5.

Katz, J.S. (2004) 'Palliative care in institutions.' In S. Payne, J. Seymour and C. Ingleton (eds) *Palliative Care Nursing: Principles and Evidence for Practice.* Milton Keynes: Open University Press.

Katz, I.R., Beaston-Wimmer, P., Parmelee, P., Friedman, E. and Lawton, M.P. (1993) 'Failure to thrive in the elderly: exploration of the concept and delineation of psychiatric components.' *Journal of Geriatric Psychiatry Neurology 6,* 151–69.

Kerr, D., Wilkinson, H. and Cunningham, C. (2008) *Supporting Older People in Care Homes at Night.* York: Joseph Rowntree Foundation.

Killeen, J. (2000) *Planning Signposts for Dementia Care Services.* Edinburgh: Alzheimer's Scotland Action on Dementia.

Kitwood, T. (1997) *Dementia Reconsidered: The Person Comes First.* Milton Keynes: Open University Press.

Knapp, M. and Prince, M. (2007) *Dementia UK: Report to the Alzheimer's Society, King's College London and London School of Economics and Political Science.* London: Alzheimer's Society.

Knauth, P. (1998) 'Innovative worktime arrangements.' *Scandinavian Journal of Work Environment and Health 24* (Suppl. 3), 13–17.

Knauth, P., Eichhorn, B., Loewenthal, I., Gaertner, K.H. and Rutenfranz, J. (1983) 'Reduction of night work by re-designing of shift rotas.' *International Archives of Occupational and Environmental Health 51,* 371–9.

Knauth, P. and Hornberger, S. (2003) 'Preventive and compensatory measures for shift workers.' *Occupational Medicine 53,* 109–16.

Knutsson, A. (2003) 'Health disorders of shift workers.' *Occupational Medicine 53,* 103–108.

Kogi, K. (1998) 'International regulations on the organization of shift work.' *Scandinavian Journal of Work Environment and Health 24* (Suppl. 3), 7–12.

Kogi, K. (2000) 'Should Shift Workers Nap? Spread, Roles and Effects of On-duty Napping.' In S. Hornberger, P. Knauth, G. Costa and S. Folkard (eds) *Shift Work in the 21st Century.* Frankfurt: Peter Lang.

Komaromy, C., Sidell, M. and Katz, J.T. (2000) 'The quality of terminal care in residential and nursing homes.' *International Journal of Palliative Nursing 6,* 4, 192–200.

Lahti, T.A., Partonen, T., Kyyronen, P., Kauppinen, T. and Pukkala, E. (2008) 'Night-time work predisposes to non-Hodgkin lymphoma.' *International Journal of Cancer 123,* 2148–51.

Landi, F., Cesari, M., Russo, A., Onder, G., Lattanzio, F. and Bernabei, R. (2003) 'Potentially reversible risk factors and urinary incontinence in frail older people living in community.' *Age and Ageing 32*, 2, 194–9.

Livingston, S. (2003) 'Effective interventions to support medicine use in older people.' *Pharmaceutical Journal 270*, 893–5.

Lloyd L. (2000) 'Dying in old age: Promoting well-being at the end of life.' *Mortality 5*, 2, 171–88.

McCaffery, M.S. (1968) *Nursing Theories Related to Cognition, Bodily Pain, and Man–Environment Interactions.* Los Angeles, CA: UCLA Students Store.

McClean, W. (2000) *Practice Guide for Pain Management for People with Dementia in Institutional Care.* Stirling: Dementia Services Development Centre.

McClean, W. and Cunningham, C. (2007) *Pain in Older People and People with Dementia: A Practice Guide.* Stirling: Dementia Services Development Centre.

McCracken, L.M. and Iverson, G.L. (2001) 'Predicting complaints of impaired cognitive functioning in patients with chronic pain.' *Journal of Pain and Symptom Management 21*, 5, 392–6.

McCullagh, P.J., Carswell, W., Augusto, J.C., Martin, S. *et al.* (2009) *State of the Art on Night-Time Care of People with Dementia.* Proceedings of the Conference on Assisted Living 2009. London: IET.

MacDonald, A.J.D. and Carpenter, G.I. (2003) 'The recognition of dementia in 'non-EMI' nursing home residents in South East England.' *International Journal of Geriatric Psychiatry 18*, 105–108.

McDonald, A.D., McDonald, J.C. and Armstrong, B. (1988) 'Prematurity and work in pregnancy.' *British Journal of Industrial Medicine 45*, 56–62.

McGrath, A.M. and Jackson, G. (1997) 'Survey of neuroleptic prescribing in residents of nursing homes in Glasgow.' *British Medical Journal 312*, 611–12.

McKeith, I., Fairbairn, A., Perry, R., Thompson, P. and Perry, E. (1992) 'Neuroleptic sensitivity in patients with senile dementia of Lewy body type.' *British Medical Journal 305*, 673–8.

McKeith, I., Mintzer, J., Aarsland, D., Burn, D. *et al.* (2004) 'Dementia with Lewy bodies.' *Lancet Neurology 3*, 1, 19–28.

McKeith, I.G., Galasko, K., Wilcock, G.K. and Byrne, E.J. (1995) 'Lewy body dementia: Diagnosis and treatment.' *British Journal of Psychiatry 1167*, 6, 709–717.

McLean, W.J. and Higginbotham, N.H. (2002) 'Prevalence of pain among nursing home residents in rural New South Wales.' *Medical Journal of Australia 177*, 17–20.

McNair, D., Pollock, R., Cunningham, C. and McGuire, B. (2010) *Light and Lighting Design for People with Dementia.* Stirling: Dementia Services Development Centre, University of Stirling.

Main, C. and Spanswick, C. (2000) *Pain Management: An Interdisciplinary Approach.* Edinburgh: Churchill Livingstone.

Mammalle, N., Laumon, E. and Lazar, P. (1984) 'Prematurity and occupational activity during pregnancy.' *American Journal of Epidemiology 119*, 309.

Manabe, K., Matsuit, T. and Yanaya, M. (2000) 'Sleep patterns and mortality among elderly patients in a geriatric hospital.' *Gerontology 46*, 318–22.

Marie Curie Cancer Care (2009) *End of Life Care for People with Dementia.* London: Marie Curie Palliative Care Research Unit.

Martin, J. (2000) 'Assessment and treatment of sleep disturbances in older adults.' *Clinical Psychology Review 20*, 6, 783–805.

Mason, D.J. (2008) 'Sleep on it: The night shift, that is.' *American Journal of Nursing 108*, 3.

Mason, J. and Scior, K. (2004) 'Diagnostic overshadowing amongst clinicians working with people with intellectual disabilities in the UK.' *Journal of Intellectual Disability Research 47* (Suppl. 1), 16–25.

Matthews, F. and Denning, T. (2002) 'Prevalence of dementia in institutional care.' *Lancet 360*, 9328, 225–6.

Meisen, B. (1993) 'Alzheimer's disease, the phenomenon of parent fixation and Bowlby's attachment theory.' *International Journal of Geriatric Psychiatry 8*, 147–53.

Miller, M. (1997) 'Fluid and electrolyte homeostasis in the elderly: Physiological changes of ageing and clinical consequences.' *Ballières Clinical Endocrinol Metabolism 11*, 367–87.

Miller, E. and Morris, R. (1993) *The Psychology of Dementia.* Chichester: John Wiley and Sons.

Morley, J. (2000) 'Water, water, everywhere and not a drop to drink.' *The Journals of Gerontology Series A: Biological Sciences and Medical Sciences 55*, M359–60.

Morley, J.E. (1999) 'An overview of diabetes mellitus in older persons.' *Clinical Geriatric Medicine 15*, 211–224.

Morley, J.E. and Kraenzle, D. (1994) 'Causes of weight loss in a community nursing home.' *Journal of the American Geriatrics Society 42*, 583–5.

Morley, J.E. and Silver, A.J. (1995) 'Nutritional issues in nursing home care.' *Annals of Internal Medicine 123*, 850–59.

Molloy, D.M. and Lubinski, R. (1995) 'Dementia: Impact and Clinical Perspectives.' In R. Lubinski (ed.) *Dementia and Communication*. San Diego, CA: Singular.

Monane, M. (1992) 'Insomnia in the elderly.' *Journal of Clinical Psychiatry 234*, 31–9.

Morin, C.M. and Espie, C.A. (2003) *Insomnia: A Clinical Guide to Assessment and Treatment*. New York: Springer.

Morrison, R. and Sui, A.L. (2000) 'A comparison of pain and its treatment in advanced dementia and cognitively intact patients with hip fracture.' *Journal of Pain and Symptom Management 19*, 4, 240–8.

Miura, S., Ito, R., Takatsuka, S. and Kunifuji, S. (2008) 'Aware group home enhanced by RFID technology.' *Proceedings of the 12th International Conference on Knowledge-Based Intelligent Information and Engineering Systems*.

Muzet, A., Nicolas, A., Tassi, P., Dewasmes, G. and Bonneau, A. (1995) 'Implementation of napping in industry and the problem of sleep inertia.' *Journal of Sleep Research 4* (Suppl. 2), 67–9.

National Sleep Foundation (2002) 'Sleep in America poll.' Available at www.sleepfoundation.org, accessed on 13 May 2010.

Nolan M., Featherston J. and Nolan J. (2003) 'Palliative care philosophy in care homes: Lessons from New Zealand.' *British Journal of Nursing 12*, 16, 974–9.

Nor, K., McIntosh, I.B. and Jackson, G.A. (2005) *Vascular Dementia: Series for Clinicians*. Stirling: Dementia Services Development Centre.

Nurminen, T. (1989) 'Shift work, fetal development and course of pregnancy.' *Scandinavian Journal of Work Environment and Health 15*, 395–403.

Ouslander, J.G., Greengold, B. and Chen, S. (1987) 'External catheter use and urinary tract infections among incontinent male nursing home patients.' *Journal of American Geriatric Society 35*, 1063–70.

Ouslander, J.G. and Schnelle, J.F. (1995) 'Incontinence in the nursing home.' *Annals of Internal Medicine 122*, 6, 438–49.

Ouslander, J.G., Schnelle, J., Simmons, S.F., Bates-Jensen, B. and Zeitlin, M. (1993) 'The dark side of incontinence: Incontinence at night in nursing homes.' *Journal of the American Geriatrics Society 41*, 371–6.

Ouslander, J.G., Schnelle, J.F., Uman, G. *et al.* (1995) 'Predictors of successful prompted voiding among incontinent nursing home residents.' *Journal of the American Medical Association 273*, 1366–70.

Palmer, M.P., Reid, B.J., Czarapata, T.J. and Newman, D.K. (1997) 'Urinary outcomes in older adults: Research and clinical perspectives.' *Urology Nursing 17*, 2–9.

Peet, S.M., Castleden, C.M., Mcgrother, C.W. and Duffin, H.M. (1996) 'The management of urinary incontinence in residential and nursing homes for older people.' *Age and Ageing 25*, 2, 139–43.

Peet, S.M., Castleden, C.M. and McGrother, C.W. (1995) 'Prevalence of urinary and faecal incontinence in hospitals and residential and nursing homes for older people.' *British Medical Journal 311*, 1063–4.

Peate, I. (2007) 'Strategies for coping with shift work.' *Nursing Standard 4*, 42–5.

Phillips, P.A., Johnston, C.I. and Gray, L. (1993) 'Disturbed fluid and electrolyte homoestasis following dehydration in elderly people.' *Age and Ageing 22*, S26–33.

Pollock, R., Mcnair, D., McGuire, B. and Cunningham, C. (2008) *Designing Lighting for People with Dementia*. Stirling: Dementia Services Development Centre.

Porock D., Oliver D.P., Zweig S., Rantz M., Mehr D., Madsen R. and Petroski G. (2005) 'Predicting death in the nursing home: Development and validation of the 6-month Minimum Data Set mortality risk index.' *Journals of Gerontology. A: Biological Sciences and Medical Sciences 60*, 491–8.

Prinz, P.N., Vitiello, M.V., Raskind, M.A. and Thorpy, M.J. (1990) 'Geriatrics: sleep disorders and aging.' *New England Journal of Medicine 323*, 8, 520–26.

Reid, K., Roberts, T. and Dawson, D. (1997) 'Improving shiftwork management II: Shiftwork and health.' *Journal of Occupational Health and Safety Australia and New Zealand 13*, 5, 439–50.

Rimmer, D.W., Boivin, D.B., Shanahan, T.L., Kronauer, R.E., Duffy, J.F. and Czeisler, C.A. (2000) 'Dynamic resetting of the human circadian pacemaker by intermittent bright light.' *American Journal of Physiology, Regulatory Integrative and Comparative Physiology 279*, 5, R1574–9.

Rogers, A.S., Holmes, S.R. and Spencer, M.B. (2001) 'The effect of shift work on driving to and from work.' *Shift International News 18*, 43.

Rosekind, M.R., Smith, R.M. and Miller, D.L. (1995) 'Alertness management: Strategic naps in operational settings.' *Journal of Sleep Research 4* (Suppl. 2), 62–6.

Royal College of Physicians (2006) *National Audit of Continence Care for Older People.* London: RCP.

Royal Commission on Long Term Care (1999) *With Respect to Old Age: Long Term Care – Rights and Responsibilities.* London: The Stationery Office.

Rüdiger, H.W. (2004) 'Health problems due to night shift work and jetlag.' *Internist (Berlin) 45*, 9, 1021–5.

Russell, R.M., Rasmussen, H. and Lichtenstein, A.H. (1999) 'Modified Food Guide Pyramid for people over seventy years of age.' *Journal of Nutrition 129*, 751–3.

Sander, R. (2002) 'Standing and moving: Helping people with vascular dementia.' *Nursing Older People 14*, 1, 20–26.

Schnelle, J.F., Alessi, C.A., Al-Samarrai, N.R. *et al.* (1999) 'The nursing home at night: Effects of an intervention on noise, light and sleep.' *Journal of American Geriatrics Society 47*, 430–38.

Schnelle, J.F., Cruise, P.A. and Alessi, C.A. (1998) 'Sleep hygiene in physically dependent nursing home residents.' *Sleep 21*, 515–23.

Schnelle, J. and Ouslander, J. (2006) 'CMS Guidelines and improving continence care in nursing homes: The role of the medical director.' *Journal of the American Medical Directors Association 7*, 2, 131–2.

Schnelle, J.F., Ouslander, J.G., Simmons, S.F., Alessi, C.A. and Gravel, M.D. (1993a) 'Nighttime sleep and bed mobility among incontinent nursing home residents.' *Journal of the American Geriatrics Society 41*, 903–9.

Schnelle, J.F., Ouslander, J.G., Simmons, S.F., Alessi, C.A. and Gravel, M. (1993b) 'The nighttime environment, incontinence care, and sleep disruption in nursing homes.' *Journal of the American Geriatrics Society 41*, 910–14.

Schochat, T., Martin, J., Marler, M. and Ancoli-Israel, S. (2000) 'Illumination levels in nursing home patients: Effects on sleep and activity rhythms.' *Journal of Sleep Research 9*, 373–9.

Schwartz, A.N. and Vogel, M.E. (1990) 'Nursing home staff and residents' families role expectations.' *Gerontologist 30*, 49–53.

Schwerha, J.J. (2005) 'Occupational medicine forum.' *Journal of Occupational and Environmental Medicine 47*, 1.

Scott, A.J. (2005) 'What recommendations can be given to shiftworkers and their employers to help cope with the effects of night work?' *Journal of Occupational and Environmental Medicine 47*, 1, 91–2.

Scottish Executive (2005) *National Care Standards: Care Homes for Older People.* Edinburgh: Scottish Executive.

Shapiro, C., Heslegrave, R.J., Beyers, J. and Picard, L. (1997) *Working the Shift: A Self-Health Guide.* Thornhill, Canada: Joli Joco Publishers.

Shephard, R.J. (1995) 'Physical activity, fitness, and health: The current consensus.' *Quest 47*, 3, 288–303.

Ship, J.A. and Fischer, D.J. (1997) 'The relationship between dehydration and parotid salivary gland function in young and older healthy adults.' *The Journals of Gerontology 52a*, M310–19.

Sidell, M. (2003) 'The Training Needs of Carers.' In J.S. Katz and S.M. Peace (eds) *End of Life in Care Homes: A Palliative Care Approach.* Oxford: Oxford University Press.

Small N., Froggat, K. and Downs, M. (2007) *Living and Dying with Dementia: Dialogues about Palliative Care.* Oxford: Oxford University Press.

Smith P. (1998) *Death and Dying in a Nursing Home.* Norwich: University of East Anglia.

Schneider, D.L. (2002) 'Safe and effective therapy for sleep problems in the older patient.' *Geriatrics 57*, 5, 24–35.

Sorbye, L.W., Finne-Soveri, H., Ljunggren, G., Topinkova, E., *et al.* (2008) 'Urinary incontinence and use of pads – clinical features and need for help in home care at 11 sites in Europe.' *Scandanavian Journal of Caring Science 23*, 33–44.

Swaen, G.M.H., van Amelsvoort, L.G.P.M., Bültmann, U. and Kant, I.J. (2003) 'Fatigue as a risk factor for being injured in an occupational accident: Results from the Maastricht Cohort Study.' *Occupational and Environmental Medicine 60* (Suppl. 1), i88–92.

Szuba, M.P., Kloss, J.D. and Dinges, D.F. (eds) (2003) *Insomnia: Principles and Management.* Cambridge: Cambridge University Press.

Tepas, D. (2000) 'Should a General Recommendation to Nap be Made to Workers?' In S. Hornberger, P. Knauth, G. Costa and S. Folkard (eds) *Shift Work in the 21st Century.* Frankfurt: Peter Lang.

Thomson, W., Brown, R.H. and Williams, S.M. (1992) 'Dentures, prosthetic treatment needs and mucosal health in an institutionalised elderly population.' *NZ Dental Journal 88*, 51–5.

Travis, S.S., Bernard, M., Dixon, S., McAuley, W.J., Loving, G. and McClanahan, L. (2002) 'Obstacles to palliation and end-of-life care in the long-term care facility.' *Gerontologist 42*, 3, 342–9.

Tsai, P. and Chang, J. (2004) 'Assessment of pain in elders with dementia.' *MedSurg Nursing 13*, 6, 364–90.

Uehata, T. and Sasakawa, N. (1982) 'The fatigue and maternity disturbances of night workwomen.' *Journal of Human Ergology (Tokyo) 11*, 465–74.

Utton, D. (2006) *Designing Homes for People with Dementia.* London: Journal of Dementia Care and Hawker Publications.

Vitiello, M.V. (2006) 'Sleep in normal aging.' *Sleep Medical Clinics 1*, 171–6.

Vitiello, M.V., Foley, D. and Stratton, K.L. (2004) 'Prevalence of sleep complaints and insomnia in the Vitamins and Lifestyle (VITAL) Study cohort of 77,000 older men and women.' *Sleep 27*, 120.

Watson, R. (1994) 'Measuring feeding difficulty in patients with dementia: replication and validation of the EdFED scale.' *Journal of Advanced Nursing 19*, 850–5.

Wedderburn, A. (ed.) (1991) *Bulletin of European Shift Work Topics No. 3: Guidelines for Shift Workers.* Dublin: European Foundation for the Improvement of Living and Working Conditions.

Weinberg, A.D., Pals, J.K., Levesque, P.G., Beal, L.F., Cunningham, T.J. and Minaker, K.L. (1994) 'Dehydration and death during febrile episodes in the nursing home.' *Journal of American Geriatrics Society 42*, 968–71.

WHO (World Health Organization) Guidelines (1996) *Cancer and Pain Relief.* Geneva: WHO.

Wilson, M.M.G. (1998) 'The management of dehydration in the nursing home.' *Facts, Research and Intervention in Geriatrics,* 181–200.

Wood, A., Vitrone, G., Doan, T., Cao, Q. *et al.* (2006) 'ALARM-NET: Wireless Sensor networks for Assisted-living and Residential Monitoring.' Technical Report CS-2006-11, Department of Computer Science, University of Virginia.

Woods, B., Keady, J. and Seddon, D. (2007) *Involving Families in Care Homes: A Relationship Approach to Dementia Care.* London: Jessica Kingsley Publishers.

Woods, P. and Ashley, J. (1995) 'Simulated presence therapy: Using selected memories to manage problem behaviors in Alzheimer's disease patients.' *Geriatric Nursing 16*, 1, 9–14.

Working Time Regulations (1998) Statutory Instrument 1998 No. 1833.

World Health Organization (2002) *National Cancer Control Programmes: Policies and Managerial Guidelines.* Second edition. Geneva: World Health Organization.

Wright, D., Chapman, N., Foundling-Miah, M. and Greenwall, R. (2006) *Consensus Guidelines on the Medication Management of Adults with Swallowing Difficulties.* Bristol: Connect Medical.

Xu, X., Ding, M., Li, B. and Christiani, D.C. (1994) 'Association of rotating shiftwork with preterm births and low birth weight among never smoking women textile workers in China.' *Journal of Occupational and Environmental Medicine 51*, 470–74.

Yoon, I.Y., Jeong, D.U., Kwon, K.B., Kang, S.B. and Song, B.G. (2002) 'Bright light exposure at night and light attenuation in the morning improve adaptation of night shift workers.' *Sleep 25*, 3, 351–6.

Zarit, S.H. and Whitlatch, C.J. (1993) 'The effects of placement in nursing homes on family caregivers: Short and long term consequences.' *Irish Journal of Psychology 14*, 25–37.

Zwakhalen, S.M.G., Hamers, J.P.H., Abu-Saad, H.H. and Berger, M.P.F. (2006) 'Pain in elderly people with severe dementia: A systematic review of behavioural pain assessment tools.' *BMC Geriatrics 6*, 3.

# Subject Index

# Author Index